Creating a
Productive
Selling
Zone®

Creating a
Productive
Selling
Zone®

John Boyens

BOYENSGROUP®
Brentwood, Tennessee
www.boyens.com

Cover and graphic design by Cindy Boyens

ISBN: 978-0-9798750-0-7

Printed in the United States of America
1 2 3 4 5 6 — 11 10 09 08 07

Contents

Introduction

Creating a Productive Selling Zone® is not some sort of rigid sales training program, formula, or methodology that reinvents the selling wheel or reprograms salespeople. Nor is it a destination that puts salespeople on a journey where they eventually step back out into the light as a new person, reshaped and recast to do things in strange ways as pre-ordained by a sales guru touting a new system that sounds like so much psychobabble.

The Productive Selling Zone® (PSZ) is not a place found on a map, but rather *a state of effectiveness*.

Elite athletes in many sports, such as golf, football, and gymnastics, often talk about "being in the zone" while in the middle of competition, where they are totally "tuned in" to doing the right things to be successful. They are not distracted by crowd noise, self-doubt, or other concerns. They are relaxed and confident, even getting to the point where they believe they will make every putt (in golf) or complete every pass (in football).

Successful salespeople know what it takes to work their way into the zone and, as importantly, what it then takes to stay there. The successes achieved in this zone, just like in sports, are measurable, in terms of wins and

> *The Productive Selling Zone® (PSZ) is not a place found on a map but rather a state of effectiveness.*

losses, as well as before and after sales metrics such as increased order size, shorter sales cycles, more competitive takeaways, sales made at higher margins, etc.

Over the years, the Boyens Group® has studied and interviewed more than fifteen thousand salespeople and their managers from a variety of industries all over the globe. Out of this, we have been able to identify certain daily traits, activities, and behaviors demonstrated among the best of the best performers today.

In addition to our best-practices research, we have interviewed thousands of companies and asked them to describe the best salesperson they've ever encountered and what it was that set him or her apart from other

> *Our tools, processes, and concepts enable salespeople to maximize their performance on a consistent basis.*

salespeople. We combined our buyer-based interview data with our best practices research to create a set of tools, processes, and concepts that we introduce in our custom programs, and speaking and consulting engagements. This book is not meant to take

the place of one of our workshops, but many of the tools, processes, and concepts we teach in our workshops form the backbone of this book.

We have found that professional sales teams rarely suffer from a lack of effort. However, the disparity between effort and positive results is quite common. So what gets in the way? Is it the marketplace? Is it the competition? Is it poor processes internally? Is it because of poor training?

We know for a fact that most companies invest in the professional development of their sales teams, but they become frustrated when the desired results are not achieved. Who can blame them? The Boyens Group® has a track record of documented successes, including helping our clients shorten their sales cycles, increase their average order size, maintain the integrity of their pricing structure, improve the size and quality of their pipelines, and increase the number of salespeople at or above plan.

> *The fact is, sales organizations are only productive when there is a convergence of effort and positive results.*

We believe that we can help any seller's game by tweaking and adjusting their selling style without resorting to some hit-and-miss extreme makeover mode of sales training. Our tools, processes, and concepts enable salespeople to maximize their performance on a consistent basis.

We are able to help our clients achieve their goals through a combination of our dynamic training programs, consulting services, speaking engagements, and sales management systems. That allows us to provide unique perspectives and powerful tools that enable sales organizations to be more productive. The fact is, sales organizations are only productive when there is a *convergence of effort and positive results.*

Real productivity in a sales process is recognizable and measurable because productive processes have specific characteristics. The balance of this book will detail those characteristics.

—John Boyens

Acknowledgments

Thank you to my family:

My wife, Cindy. This book would never have been published without her!

My mother and father, Betty and Bob Boyens, for their support and unwavering belief in me.

My children, Ryan and Brent, for keeping life interesting.

A special thank-you to:

My friend and colleague, Merrylue Martin, for helping to create the tools, processes, and concepts introduced in this book and that serve as the backbone of our workshops.

Mike Towle, for helping me put my thoughts on paper.

All of my associates, friends, coworkers, and clients that have shared their experiences with me. Their input continues to be invaluable to our success.

Creating a
Productive
Selling
Zone®

1
Four Reasons Why People Don't Buy

"I don't need that."

"I don't have the budget."

"Your price is too high."

"I can get the same thing from Company X."

"We'll get back to you."

"Call me next month."

"That's great. Can you send me something?"

"We've always done it this way."

"I'll run it past my boss."

Have you ever heard any of those words come out of your prospect's mouth? If you've been in sales for any length of time, of course you have! If you want to be productive in sales, the first thing you have to know is *why* people don't buy! Notice I said "people" versus "companies," because we have found that people buy from people, not companies!

THE FOUR REASONS WHY PEOPLE DON'T BUY

1. No need. The prospect says that they don't need your product or service. What they really mean is that

1

they don't *perceive* that they need it. They believe that someone else is fulfilling that need or that they are buying it from somebody else or that they are able to satisfy their requirements internally.

2. No vision. They are unwilling to (or choose not to) *look at a new way* of doing something, or they don't believe that your company has the products or capability to deliver.

3. No value. They can't *cost justify* or *value justify* the decision to buy your product or service. The good news is that they usually give you a clue early in the sales cycle that value hasn't been established when they ask, "How much is it?" or "What does it cost?" The disconnect between the prospect and the seller occurs when the salesperson is talking about the product or service before *need* has been admitted or *vision* has been created.

4. No power. Salespeople spend an inordinate amount of time selling to people who can't buy. It's always important to find the person (or the people) with the *power of the pen*.

As a matter of fact, we continue to hear the following recurring themes from sales managers across the globe:

- *"My salespeople have a difficult time getting to the decision makers, so they waste their time talking to the wrong people."*

- *"On those rare occasions when my salespeople do get to the decision maker, they engage in reactive, tactical conversations with their prospects versus proactive, strategic conversations."*

- "My salespeople have a hard time cost-justifying our solutions, so they have a tendency to sell more on price than value."

- "My salespeople have a difficult time differentiating themselves from our competition, so our products often become commoditized."

We refer to these behaviors as *unproductive selling characteristics*.

NAVIGATE THE THREE STAGES OF BUYING

There are three stages of buying. They are the **Need phase**, the **Proof phase**, and the **Risk phase**. So how can salespeople successfully navigate the three stages?

Moving the Prospect Through the NEED Phase

1. **Identify the key players.**

2. **Uncover their needs or business problems by asking situational or behavioral questions.** (For example: How do you go about penetrating a new market? How can you ensure your new product launch will be successful?)

3. **Understand the competitive landscape.** (For example: Who's their current supplier? How do they operate today?)

4. **Identify the costs of doing things the way they do it today—*both hard and soft costs*.** (For example: time, money, resources, etc.)

5. **Understand how your prospects make decisions and their rules of engagement.** (For example: can they sign a contract or do they have to put out a bid? Are you able to entertain your prospects or do you have to keep your distance?)

Moving the Prospect Through the PROOF Phase

1. Use references, testimonials, and customer success stories to enhance your credibility.
2. Show them how you can help them solve their business problems and make them a *hero*.
3. Provide cost justification (Return on Investment).
4. Differentiate yourself from your competition.

Moving the Prospect Through the RISK Phase

1. Remind them of the financial impact and make sure you calculate the *cost* of delay or the *cost* of "no decision."
2. Identify the *successes* that they can gain— (such as improving market share, increasing revenue, and improving profitability).
3. Identify the *consequences* if they take no action. In other words, what bad things will happen to them if they don't make the decision to go with your company? Remind them that their business problems won't go away unless they take action to do something different.

Kevin Brown, a Boyens Group® client and Executive Vice President of Sales for Yankelovich, explains why you can't always believe it when a prospect says he doesn't have the budget to buy your product or service:

"What my sales team hears most frequently is, 'We have no budget.' John's training has helped us not to accept the 'no budget' excuse, but rather to focus on creating value for the prospect. For example, one time we were dealing with a VP of marketing at a consumer packaged-goods company who told us there was no budget and to come back before the start of the next fiscal year. We had taken the VP through BIO® and VALU Builder®, and we were able to identify a new product initiative that was incredibly important to sales growth. We convinced the client that a concept review by our consulting staff would mitigate some of the risks with rolling out a new product. He agreed: Even with 'no budget,' he spent $25,000 on this initial engagement!"

GOOD COMMUNICATION EQUALS SUCCESS

Ninety percent of all selling problems stem from poor communication. It could be poor questioning skills, poor listening skills, poor documentation skills, or just a case of "happy ears" where salespeople hear what they want to hear versus what the prospect actually says. In any event, the most successful salespeople ask questions to verify the business issues, help their prospects analyze the impact of those issues, and link their unique capabilities, all before they ever unveil proof!

SUMMARY OF KEY POINTS
(Chapter 1)

- The Productive Selling Zone® is a *state of effectiveness*, not a destination.

- People buy from people.

- The four reasons people don't buy are no need, no vision, no value, and no power.

- The three stages of buying are the Need phase, the Proof phase, and the Risk phase.

- Communication skills are the key to your success. Don't unveil proof unless need has been admitted, that need has been measured, and a new vision has been created.

2
Buying Behaviors

Not all buyers are the same, an obvious maxim in sales that goes well beyond the usual distinguishing factors such as personality type, size of wallet, or whether they prefer a conference room or a restaurant table for transacting business. It is important to be able to differentiate one buying type from another so that you will know exactly how to move someone from prospect to client. While there are a number of categories of buyers, I'd like to focus on the three most common:

1. The Risk-Averse Buyer. This is the buyer who knows that there is a specific need to be filled but is having a problem pulling the trigger. They don't want to take chances, believing instead that it is always better to be safe than sorry. The five characteristics of a Risk-Averse Buyer are:

1. They are afraid of making mistakes.

2. They're usually very analytical.

3. They're afraid of "buyer's remorse."

4. They express worry about what other people will think.

5. They start asking questions about what happens if what they are buying doesn't work.

The best way to sell to a risk-averse buyer is to be able to identify the consequences of staying where they are. In other words, the risk of *no decision*. To put it more bluntly, what are some of the bad things that might happen if they don't make the decision to buy from you?

2. The Egocentric Buyer. This type of buyer can be spotted from a mile away. These are the people with the huge desk, very proud of themselves. They wear the best clothing and drive the hottest car, and their egos are very important to them. It is not hard to get them to talk about themselves; just let 'em go. Many times they will save you the trouble of trying to talk them into buying from you—let them do the work for you.

When it is your turn to talk, the best way to sell to ego-based buyers is to show them what successes they can gain by purchasing your product or service. For instance: better results, a promotion, larger bonuses, their name in lights, etc.

Show them how they could be the first in their industry to buy your product or service, and document the competitive advantage that they will receive in return. Remember, they are seeking affirmation about their status or ideas as much as they are seeking your best deal. Make them feel important.

3. The Price-Based Buyer. Price-based buyers have been around since the beginning of time and always will be. To hear them speak, you'd think that all they are looking for is the cheapest possible price that you or a competitor can offer them.

The good news is that price-based buyers don't exist. Not really. The bad news is that there are many who *believe* they are price-based. They want the best deal, the lowest price, and preferred terms, and your job is to bring them full circle to see the value of your products or services.

When a price-based buyer starts talking about cutting your price, that's when you need to be able to work ROI (Return on Investment) into your conversations in a way that the buyer understands. Many salespeople get stuck on how to make that transition of going from a buyer's mention of price to explaining ROI, but it's really quite simple.

You can't offer an ROI on your product or service unless you know what it costs them to do business *without* your product or service. Further, you can't offer an ROI unless you know what benefits they will realize once they purchase your product or service. Once you know those two variables, then you are able to say very clearly, "If you spend X, you'll be able to generate Y in return in less than ninety days!"

> *You can't offer an ROI on your product or service unless you know what it costs them to do business without your product or service.*

In the early '90s I was accompanying one of my salesman who was working his territory in Northern California. We visited a prospect who appeared to get a great deal of pleasure beating up my salesperson over price. Over and over, this prospect just kept talking about price. For twenty minutes all we heard was price, price, price, and price. My salesperson tried repeatedly to shift the conversation from price but was unsuccessful.

It got to where I couldn't hold back any longer, so I decided to jump in. I said to this person, "It seems to me that you are a price-based buyer, right?" And with a certain amount of glee, he sat up straight in his chair, stuck out his chest, and said, "Yes, I buy exclusively on price!"

I said, "Really? Well, I'm just curious. What kind of car do you drive?"

He said, "A Honda Accord."

I said, "Why don't you drive a Yugo?"

He said, "Because a Honda Accord has a better service record and gets better gas mileage."

So, then I said, "Well, I guess it's not always about price."

—John Boyens

Other buying behaviors include:

Loyalty-based: These are the buyers who have been buying from the same vendors for a hundred years (give or take). So how do you sell to loyalty-based buyers? Focus first on building up your own credentials with success stories, testimonials, and customer references. Tell them of the long-term relationships you've established with others. Give them specifics to let them know that they can count on you!

Value-based: These are the easiest buyers to sell to. They put functionality ahead of ego, and they have no qualms about paying a price higher than your competitor's as long as you can value-justify your product or service. The best way to sell to them is to help them quantify the value—the before-and-after picture.

A good salesperson knows how to sell value over price, and the value-based buyers give you the opportunity to speak their language.

Convenience-based: These buyers are looking to do business with someone who makes it easy to do business with them. Some examples of how to make it easy to do business include offering them:

- 24/7 customer service
- Online capabilities
- Variety of payment options
- Talking with a "live" person
- Number of locations
- Product/service guarantees
- Multi-year pricing
- Volume discounts
- Good return policy

11

These guidelines concerning buyer behaviors will help you work with many types of people. However, there will be times when a single buyer will exhibit two or more of these behaviors. The key to your success will be identifying the predominant behavior and then managing expectations.

> *It is crucial with most prospects that you discuss Return on Investment (ROI) with them. This is a concept emphasized throughout this book, because you need to know how to quantify investments in such a way that the prospect just doesn't have to take your word for how good your product or service is—he or she can recognize it.*

It is crucial with most prospects that you discuss Return on Investment (ROI) with them. This is a concept emphasized throughout this book, because you need to know how to quantify investments in such a way that the prospect just doesn't have to take your word for how good your product or service is—he or she can recognize it.

The best way to work with ROI is to use *their* numbers; don't make up or rough out your own. They will grasp the numbers better if they have ownership of them. If they don't have the numbers at their fingertips, walk them through the process. For example:

- How many marketing campaigns do you plan to launch next year?
- How many pieces will you mail per campaign?
- What are your costs per piece?
- What's your targeted response rate?

- What's your historical response rate from previous campaigns?

- What percentage of your mail is undeliverable?

- What would a half percent improvement in response rate mean to you?

By asking these types of questions, you will be able to help your prospects *measure the cost* of doing business the way they do it today and, as importantly, see the value of doing business with your company.

SUMMARY OF KEY POINTS
(Chapter 2)

- Not all buyers are the same.

- Once you uncover a prospect's predominant buying behavior, all you have to do is manage expectations.

- Good salespeople ask situational or behavioral questions to get prospects to reveal their predominant buying behavior.

- The three most common buying behaviors found in business-to-business settings are the risk-averse buyer, the egocentric buyer, and the price-based buyer.

- Other buying behaviors include the loyalty-based buyer, the value-based buyer, and the convenience-based buyer.

- Some buyers will exhibit more than one buying behavior. Don't let that throw you. Uncover their predominant buying behavior and then manage their expectations.

- Productive selling requires a return on investment (ROI) conversation between the buyer and the seller before the buyer can commit to buy.

- Use your *prospect's numbers* to make the sale for you!

3

Targeting Your Prospects

The most successful salespeople prospect all the time, and they vary the methods they use to prospect. Selected prospecting methods include generating "warm" referrals, buying mailing lists, the telephone, direct mail letters, emails, video e-mails, trade shows, chamber events, and all other forms of business-networking opportunities. They also do a very good job in segmenting their existing customer base. Successful salespeople have a plan to bring focus to what they are doing. By focusing, they can actually identify the right prospects rather than using the whole world as their prospect pool.

There are different ways to approach how you target your prospects, and some methods are more effective than others. You should start by identifying what your "best" customers look like. In other words, if your "best" customers are based in the

> *Successful salespeople have a plan to bring focus to what they are doing. By focusing, they can actually identify the right prospects rather than using the whole world as their prospect pool.*

Northwest, are involved in the manufacture of paper, have between 500 and 1,000 employees, and post annual net revenues in the $50-$100 million range, then it makes sense to prospect to all businesses that fit those same criteria.

Believe it or not, there are far too many salespeople who don't do a good job of profiling their existing accounts.

To ensure success in targeting "like" customers, ask yourself the following questions about your "best" customers:

- What industries are they in?

- What products or services do they buy from you?

- What products or services do they buy from your competitor?

- What kind of revenue stream do they have?

- How many employees do they have?

- How many locations do they have, and where are they?

- What job title or functional area made the decision to buy from you? Successful salespeople have a plan to bring focus to what they are doing. By focusing, they can actually identify the right prospects rather than using the whole world as their prospect pool.

⌖

THE FOUR-W STRATEGY

The PSZ takes targeting a step further with what we call the Four-W Strategy. In targeting your prospects, it's not only important to know what your best prospects look like, but also to know what your prospects see when they look at you.

The Four-W Strategy puts you in a good position to know your prospects in such a way as to position you

---

The Four W's

1. Who is it you are targeting? (What industries? What markets? What job functions or job titles do you sell to?)

2. What product or service are you trying to sell to them?

3. Why will they buy? (What's in it for them? Why will they use what you are selling them?)

4. What will keep them from buying from you?

---

to "win" more business, more quickly.

When communicating why the prospect would buy your product or service, it is helpful to be able to articulate your company's unique value proposition (UVP). You might have heard this referred to as "an elevator pitch." In other words, what would you say to a prospect when riding two floors on an elevator with them? It may be referred to as a unique selling proposition (USP).

> *A UVP is normally one or two sentences that identify what it is that your company does that your competition doesn't do, can't do, or won't do in the marketplace.*

A UVP is normally one or two sentences that identify what it is that your company does that your competition doesn't do, can't do, or won't do in the marketplace. Companies that can articulate their unique value proposition are able to:

17

- Differentiate themselves from their competition
- Grow market share
- Increase customer satisfaction
- Maintain margins
- Outsmart the competition

Once you've established your UVP, test it. Substitute the name of a competitor in place of your company name in your UVP. If the statement is still true, then it's not *your* UVP! In the space below, create your own UVP.

Your UVP
_____
_____
_____
_____
_____

PROSPECT PROFILES

Targeting prospects is a never-ending function of the sales process. All it takes is the willingness to implement the targeting strategies to continually build your pipeline.

Constant shifts in the marketplace brought on by factors such as companies starting up or closing, changes in consumer behavior, the effect of news events on the economy, etc., are among the hundreds of reasons that keep things changing. Your prospects are always moving, changing, and evolving. That means that your targeting efforts are never done.

Identify your existing customers' characteristics and use that information as a basis for finding new prospects that fit your profile. This will enable you to gain market share.

Depending on which business information database you use—it could be Dun and Bradstreet, Experian, InfoUSA, etc.—there are sixteen to twenty million businesses in the United States (depending on whose database you believe). That includes small businesses, at-home businesses, and so on. Subtract the number of customers you have from twenty million and the difference is your *delta of opportunity*.

There's no way you can go after all of them at the same time with the same energy. So what you do is come up with criteria to whittle down that delta-of-opportunity list to a more manageable number. Maybe you should start by identifying what *doesn't* belong on your opportunity list, such as schools, churches, or other nonprofit businesses.

The criteria used to pare down the list are often called "selects" in the direct-marketing industry. These "selects" could include SICs (standard industry classifications) and vertical markets. They could include geographic markets, employee numbers, revenue, or zip codes. The more you can pare down your list, the better your target list will be, resulting in closing more business.

> *Think quality of prospects, not quantity. Rock-solid "selects" will help take care of that for you.*

Think *quality* of prospects, not *quantity*. Rock-solid "selects" will help take care of that for you.

Salespeople need to track the results of their prospecting efforts. For instance, how many hours do they devote to prospecting per week? How many calls do they make? How often do they get to talk with the decision maker? What percentage of calls led to a follow-up action? Most sales professionals are not really good at the administrative part of the job. If you fall into that category, this is your wakeup call.

SUMMARY OF KEY POINTS
(Chapter 3)

- Successful salespeople never stop prospecting. They have a plan and a strategy to bring focus to what they are doing.

- To better know what your best future prospects look like, it is important to know identifying characteristics shared by your current customer base.

- The Four-W Strategy is a simple process that allows you to quickly assess what your company does best at the same time it assesses your prospects' needs.

- Companies that can articulate their unique value proposition are able to grow market share, increase customer satisfaction, maintain margins, and outsmart the competition.

- Knowing how to target your prospects will help you quantify and segment your prospect pool.

- By using properly identified "selects," you can quickly and effectively target only the prospective customers who fit your skill sets, resulting in closing more business. Think *quality* of prospects, not *quantity*.

4

Pipeline Development

Once you've targeted your prospects, the next step is to develop your pipeline. That involves contacting your targeted suspects and then qualifying or disqualifying them as prospects.

PRE-CALL PLANNING

Once you've qualified your prospects and started setting up meetings, you must utilize a formal pre-call planning process. Prospects become frustrated quite quickly with salespeople who have not done their homework. *Please be aware that the drive to the appointment or the walk to the boardroom does not count as pre-call planning!* It's actually done in advance of the call.

It's important for salespeople to ask two questions: "What is it that I need to know before I go out on this call?" and "Where do I go to find that information?"

Some places to find information about the prospect:

- Business section of the newspaper
- Local business journals
- Trade publications

- Industry Websites
- Prospect's Website
- Business databases such as Dun & Bradstreet, Experian, Equifax, InfoUSA, Hoover's, etc.

What you are looking for:
- Uncover the key players
- Products or services offered
- Whether the company is publicly or privately held
- Revenue size
- Number of employees
- Existing supplier relationships
- Their partners or strategic alliances
- Has this company been a client of yours in the past? And, have any individuals there been clients of yours at a previous company?

It's also important in pre-call planning to recognize that there must be at least three objectives on every call. For example, on your first "in person" call, I would suggest the following three objectives:

1. Identify the key decision makers
2. Uncover needs
3. Discover the competitive landscape

Three more things to be thinking about during the pre-call planning:

1. What needs might the prospect have that match up with my solutions (products or services)?

2. What am I going to say in my professional opening?

3. What references do I have that I can use during the call to show my credibility and expertise?

To further assist you on the subject of pre-call planning, on the next page we present a sample pre-call planning form that we created for our clients.

You'll notice that there is a section for inserting a Credibility WINdow© story (introduced in Chapter 11). Below the Credibility WINdow© section, there is a section for additional information. This can include introducing a new product line, leasing new space, divesting of a product line, or new hires.

Pre-Call Planning Form

Initial Contact	Name: Referred by: Title/Function: Company:
History with my company	
Objectives of this call	
Potential Needs	
Solution Targeting	
Opening	
Credibility WINdow©	Introduction: Reasons: Goals: Outcome:
Additional Information	

○══╼══○

PROSPECTING OVER THE TELEPHONE

Most people do not like prospecting over the telephone because of a fear of rejection. It's not fun being told *no* over the telephone.

When prospecting over the telephone, what you say needs to be quick, targeted, and engaging. Our research shows that you have fifteen to eighteen seconds to get someone's attention. That doesn't mean that you talk faster or louder!

Before making your first call, it is important to master three basic telephone skills:

1. Rate of Speech. If you speak too fast, you will tend to lose the customer and, therefore, the call objective. Speak too slowly, on the other hand, and you will bore the person on the other end. Again, the call objective has been compromised. Work toward a rate of speech of 180 to 190 words a minute. This will allow your customer to understand what you are saying; therefore, he or she will maintain interest. This is the same rate of speech taught to and used by most radio and television commentators. A good way to test your rate of speech is to cut an article out of your newspaper or use a document that contains 180 to 190 words. Then practice reading that article while timing yourself. You should get comfortable reading that article or document in one minute.

2. Volume of Speech. It is important to speak at a volume that allows the other person to hear what you are saying. The ideal volume would be similar to what you would use in conversing to someone seated across the table from you at lunch. Speak too loudly and you

7

will annoy the person on the other end of the phone as he moves the handset away from his ear. Speak too softly, on the other hand, and the person on the other end will quickly lose interest.

3. Inflection, Technique, and Control of Speech. A monotone won't cut it, and that can easily be the predicament you create for yourself when you "read" your script. The voice of confidence, knowledge, and experience is one that has a natural inflection (up and down), tonal quality, and emphasis on key words. Take it too far, though, where you start sounding like a TV infomercial pitchman or anchorman (think of Will Ferrell in *Anchorman: The Legend of Ron Burgundy*) and you'll come across as a boor. Be relaxed but enthusiastic, prepared to converse and convince, and the rest will fall into place. A good way to practice is to leave yourself a voice message with your prospecting script. Listen to the voicemail and evaluate your rate of speech, volume, inflection, and tone.

> *Be relaxed but enthusiastic, prepared to converse and convince, and the rest will fall into place.*

Another one of the key factors in successful telephone prospecting is confidence. That comes from the belief in the product or service you are selling and a genuine understanding about how the product or service will be used to the benefit of the buyer.

To be prepared for those eighteen (or fewer) seconds of over-the-phone opportunity, salespeople are advised to use the first pane of what we call the Credibility WINdow© (more on this tool in chapter 11)

28

to create an approach likely to engage the prospect. Let's look at suggested scripts for two types of calls that can be made: a cold call and a warm call. You'll substitute your information in the underlined areas. Tweaking a word here and there to better fit personal preference is encouraged if it provides an added layer of comfort, just as long as the basic meaning isn't altered:

A Cold-Call Script

"Hi, this is (<u>your first name</u>). I have been working with several (<u>same job title/industry as new prospect</u>), who have been having difficulty with (<u>describe a matching problem</u>). I'm curious if you're experiencing anything similar and if you would like to know how others in your industry have overcome this challenge?"

A Warm-Call Script

"Hi, this is (<u>your first and last name</u>). We have not had the pleasure of meeting, but (<u>person who referred you</u>) suggested that I give you a call. I have been working with several (<u>same job title/industry as new prospect</u>), who have been having difficulty with (<u>describe a matching problem</u>). I'm curious if you're experiencing anything similar and if you would like to know how they were able to overcome this challenge?"

Whether it's a cold call or a warm call, our research shows that you can expect one of several responses that you need to be prepared to address. Here are the four most common prospect responses, each followed by a good comeback to keep things moving forward.

Potential Responses:	What You Should Say:
1. Anything positive.	Ask for an appointment or keep the conversation going by sharing the rest of your Credibility WINdow©.
2. "I don't have that problem."	Come back with other challenges you often see. Have two or three prepared and ready to use.
3. "Send me something."	"Sure, may I ask you a few questions to better understand what to send you?"
4. "Not interested."	"Could you tell me who in your organization would be responsible for addressing this (<u>restate the difficulty</u>)?"

To make scripting work over time, you must track your successes and failures. As mentioned earlier in the book, measure the number of calls that you make. Count the number of times you were able to reach a "live" person. Track the number of times that your scripts led to a follow-up call or appointment. Setting time aside in your weekly planner for prospecting and for tracking your results allows you to better allocate your time and maximize your performance.

Make sure that you are prepared with good answers to all response contingencies, and be positive with your expectations. Prospecting is like the adage in the Nike commercial—"Just do it." Believe that every prospecting call you make is leading you closer to a sale.

So, scripting is important. Measuring and tracking is important. So is scheduling time on your calendar. Plan on a minimum of one hour per day for prospecting.

Let's look at some other prospecting methodologies, all with an eye toward further building the pipeline of qualified prospects.

◦═◆═◦

DIRECT MAIL

Direct mail remains a tried and true method of contacting potential customers. It gives you a great chance to grab the recipients' interest because you can relate to their business problems and, more importantly, give them hope in being able to solve those problems.

We have been doing direct-mail letters for years. In that time, it's never been enough for us to know how well they work—we also want to know *why*. It wasn't good enough that recipients responded; I wanted to figure out what made them respond so that I could isolate the reasons, replicate them in future letters, and then be able to teach this to others, as I'm doing right now.

There are three ingredients that go into making a direct-mail letter as effective as it can be:

1. **Get right to the point of describing their business challenges in bullets.** It's always easy to understand bullet points (provided they've been carefully researched and written), and it shows potential clients that you know what is going on in their world.

2. **Explain what your company does in, literally, one sentence.** Your UVP would be a good insert in your letter.

3. **Explain exactly what you can do for them.** Then give them a call-to-action with a response deadline to give them the motivation to respond quickly. We like to use ten days.

Here's a sample letter that we have used successfully to help generate leads via direct mail.

Direct Mail Sample

June 6, XXXX

Ms. Sally Smith
President
XYZ Company
123 Main Street
Anywhere, US 12345

Dear Sally:

Over the years the Boyens Group has had the opportunity to work with many Presidents and Vice Presidents of Sales and Marketing, and we continue to hear the following recurring themes:

- "My salespeople have a difficult time getting to decision makers, so they spend an inordinate amount of time selling to people who can't buy."

- "On those rare occasions when my salespeople do get to the decision maker, they engage in reactive, tactical conversations versus proactive, strategic conversations."

- "My salespeople have a hard time cost justifying our solutions, so they have a tendency to sell more on price than value."

- "My salespeople have a difficult time differentiating themselves from our competition, so our products often become commoditized."

- "Sales cycles are getting longer, and those decision-making delays are devastating."
- "Our marketing and sales departments are out of alignment."

Assuming that you face some of these issues as well, please allow me to formally introduce you to the Boyens Group. We are in the business of helping our clients:

- Improve the performance of their sales team
- Increase the effectiveness of their management team
- Optimize their business strategy at both the account and market level

We invite you to take a hard look at your organization to see if there is an opportunity to improve your sales productivity, management effectiveness, or account strategy. To prove our value, we are offering a complimentary assessment of your people, processes, and programs to identify any potential gaps that may inhibit your organization from reaching your next level of success. To take advantage of our special offer, please call me within the next ten business days at (615) 776-1257 or e-mail me at john@boyens.com.

Respectfully,

John Boyens
President

Direct mail works best when you don't flood your target market with too many letters. We suggest sending twenty-five letters every other month, using mailing lists compiled from your work in researching prospects to be targeted. It's fairly easy to measure percentages when you are dropping twenty-five letters at a time, and the best way to start is by picking specific industries. Again your target-prospect research will help you immensely here.

Your letters don't need to be exactly the same, either. Customize them. You can tweak a sentence or two to focus or to personalize the letter to a specific company or industry.

The bottom line is that a successful direct-mail piece can become a great tool in terms of establishing your credibility.

◦━━◆━━◦

E-MAIL

One thing that sets the e-mail approach apart from direct mail is that you have even less time to grab your readers' attention. With e-mails you are writing for short attention spans, so you need to get right to the point. In fact, you want their full attention even before they get to the first sentence of the e-mail's body of text. That's the importance of the subject line of the e-mail, a topic about which a whole workshop could be devised.

In today's business climate, we all get inundated with e-mails. Yet, sending them out is a necessary way of soliciting and doing business in this day and age. One rule of thumb that works here is what has been

35

referred to as the 3/3 rule, meaning it is wise to compose an e-mail letter that is three paragraphs, each one no more than three sentences in length. The reader would like to get in, get out, and be done in forty-five seconds.

When composing an e-mail, there are many things to keep in mind. Some of the do's and don'ts for sending marketing e-mails include:

- Don't send an attachment, because it won't get past the receiver's firewall.

- Don't embed photos or other types of art or graphics. That will cause your e-mail to fail to get through the firewall and might take a long time to open at the other end.

- Whenever possible, use bullet points to catch the reader's attention.

- Take great pains to make sure your subject line will be one the recipient(s) find interesting, thought provoking, or relevant.

On the following page is a sample e-mail that we wrote to generate leads:

Sample E-mail

Subject Line: Sales Growth Point Person

Can you please point me to the person in your organization who is most responsible for sales growth?

I would like to forward some information about our sales and sales management processes, which promises to boost the performance of your sales team by driving new business development as well as improving cross-selling to your existing clients. Over the years we have had the opportunity to help over 15,000 salespeople and their managers achieve their business goals.

Our programs increase the effectiveness of your sales team by identifying specific traits, behaviors, and daily activities that enable each salesperson to create a competitive advantage in their marketplace by using proactive and preemptive selling strategies.

We accomplish this by delivering sales and sales management programs based upon your individual products, market requirements, and culture. In addition, we work with your existing training programs to enable you to increase sales, improve productivity, and accelerate revenue performance.

Putting me in touch with the right person will be much appreciated and will likely help us both.

Best regards,
John Boyens
President
Boyens Group
(615) 776-1257

꘎━━✦━━꘎

TRADE SHOWS (AND HOW TO LEVERAGE THEM)

Trade shows are less about transacting business onsite and more about marketing your product or services while putting a face and a handshake with a name. A trade show can be a valuable prospecting tool if you take the initiative to follow it up.

If you are already exhibiting at trade shows, or at least actively attending them, you have a lot of company. Statistics show that more than fourteen million businesses in the United States spend billions of dollars a year on trade shows. Unfortunately, many of those businesses have continued to have a difficult time calculating their Return on Investment (ROI) or Return on Objective (ROO) for the money they spend on trade shows.

It is important that you determine which trade shows your company should attend, and you make that decision based on logic and not emotion. You want to make sure you make the best use of your booth design and setup, and devise the right post-show activities that will help drive revenue in the near term.

Over the years, most marketing executives have complained about one or more of the following problems:

1. Our marketing efforts and trade show strategies are not yielding the desired results.

2. Our market messaging is often unclear and inconsistent, so it doesn't accurately reflect our desired image.

3. We're not seeing enough of the right people at our booth, and booth traffic is down from past years.

38

One tactic that works well in advance of the trade show is contacting the show's organizers and getting a list of past attendees. This isn't necessarily getting individuals' names, but rather a list of companies and titles of attendees to find out if this show is a good fit for you. Once you've decided to attend a specific show, e-mail an invitation to your booth, some kind of activity, a new announcement, something that's a surprise, a giveaway, whatever it may be to get them to your booth.

Fewer than 20 percent of the companies that exhibit at trade shows follow up on the leads generated from the trade shows. Just by following up, even if it means dumping collected business cards out of the fishbowl and sending out a post-show letter, you are a step ahead of more than 80 percent of your competition.

Tips to Maximize Your Trade Show Budget

- Ask for a list of past attendees from the previous year's show.

- Ask for a pre-registration list and mail (or e-mail) an invitation to come to your booth (or an event).

- Prior to the trade show, make sure that your salespeople set appointments to meet with prospects and/or customers at the trade show (i.e., breakfast, lunch, dinner, drinks, golf, etc.).

- Offer to deliver a keynote address or facilitate a workshop during the trade show (in exchange for free registration, a bigger booth, or a better location on the floor).

- Create custom notepads for people working the booth that contain a place to staple a business card as well as a place to write notes about their interaction with customers/prospects.

- Always do a post-show mailer to all attendees (not just those who came by your booth).

There are other methods to developing the pipeline, such as educational forums, advertising, chambers of commerce, and white papers. What they all have in common is a prerequisite for due diligence in the form of research. Ample research of your target prospects must be conducted to establish your own credibility as a salesperson.

SUMMARY OF KEY POINTS
(Chapter 4)

- The best salespeople prospect all the time.

- The three basic telephone skills involved in enhancing your message are rate of speech, volume, and inflection/tone.

- Prospecting requires a discipline to be done on a weekly basis as well as being tracked and modified as needed.

- It's not enough to know that direct mail works but also to know why it works. Composed correctly, a direct-mail piece will entice prospects to respond quickly.

- Make sure your subject line will be one the recipient(s) find interesting, thought provoking, or relevant.

- Effective e-mail directs its recipient to put you in touch with the person to whom you need to talk.

- The trade shows that work best for you are the ones that you aggressively prepare for so you can get your core message across to those who visit your booth.

5
Getting Past the Gatekeeper(s)

No one ever said it was going to be easy getting to the decision maker.

There are many obstacles along the way, the biggest of which is the gatekeeper. A gatekeeper is a person or device placed in your path to make it difficult for you to establish contact with someone who's in a position of authority or responsibility and doesn't want to allow much access.

The three most common types of gatekeepers are receptionist, voicemail, and administrative assistant. The first and the third types might sound like one and the same. Each serves a specific function unique from the other, whether it's prioritizing incoming phone calls (the receptionist) or guarding a particular manager's or executive's time (the administrative assistant). Knowing how to deliver your message to suit each is important in getting past that gatekeeper and making a connection with your targeted prospect.

You never get a second chance to make a first impression.

> *The idea here is to treat this person with respect and take good notes so the next time you call them you can reference something from your previous call.*

So the idea here is to treat this person with respect and take good notes so the next time you call them you can reference something from your previous call.

We teach a formula to get to the decision maker that involves three major steps:

1. Start by sending a direct-marketing letter, e-mail, or video e-mail as an introduction, with the intent of generating some curiosity or interest. End that letter or e-mail with a call to action in which they can contact you, or say that you will contact them in a certain period of time not to exceed ten business days.

2. Then call within that specified time period mentioned in the initial letter. If you get voicemail, leave a message using the telephone script from Chapter 4. Don't ask them to call you back, because most of the time they won't do it anyway. It is better to say that you will give them a call back on a certain day and at a certain time.

3. Get to a live person. Call at the designated time. One of two things will happen: You'll either get that person, in which case you should engage him or her, or you'll get voicemail or the receptionist. If you get the voicemail, then try to zero out (hit "O," "*" or "#" on the keypad) to get to a receptionist or secretary, and say the following:

    "I'm wondering if you can help me." (It's in most people's nature to try and help when asked.) When they respond positively, say, "I sent John Smith a letter ten days ago, but I'm sure he gets a lot of correspondence. I was wondering if I could

> send you a copy of that letter, and then if
> you think it's of interest, could you sched-
> ule a time for John to talk with me?"

More often than not, they will say, "If I can," or "Sure, whatever I can do." That's especially true if you get through to the receptionist or the executive assistant's secretary. I think it's in their DNA to want to help people. Always remember to smile while you're asking (they can "hear" you smile over the phone).

Ask if they would prefer that you fax or e-mail the original letter to them.

This approach does work! I once sold a $300,000 contract in under fourteen days by using this approach with an international company that met me for the first time when I landed in Dublin, Ireland, to facilitate their first workshop.

❀

Let's take a step back to all this and look at the three major types of gatekeepers in a bit more detail:

1. Voicemail. This form seems to be the most prevalent for all industries. Do not hang up when you get directed to voicemail. The most common explanation given by those who hang up is something along the lines of "Look, I didn't want to leave a message, so I hung up." That's not productive or professional.

So, what should you do? Treat it as a cold call, and use that script you created when you get to the part of the voicemail that allows you to leave a message. However, there is one part of your script that you should leave out of the voicemail message—the part when you give your phone number with the "Please call me" tagline at the end. Saying that makes you sound just like any other salesperson, giving the folks at the other end an easy rationale for never returning your call.

End your voicemail with "I'll give you a call back Thursday morning at eight o'clock to follow up on this message. If you'd like to call me back before then, here's my number." This way you can control that next engagement.

2. The Executive Assistant. With the executive assistant, you normally get one of those challenging questions along the lines of "Who's calling, please?" or "Can I tell him/her what this is regarding?" That's their script.

What do you do in such a scenario? Begin with the premise that this person understands what's going on in their boss's world . . . use your script to generate interest.

It's a good idea to always put notes in your database regarding your interaction with the executive assistant so that when you're making the follow-up phone call, you will remember that a son or daughter just went off to college, or perhaps somebody got married, or there is a new baby. This allows you to personalize your next contact.

3. The Receptionist. One big difference between the executive assistant and the receptionist is that the former is just one link removed from the key person to whom you wish to speak, while the latter is typically two or three steps removed. With the receptionist, then, your goal is different from the executive assistant. The receptionist can be a source of basic company information, helping you to fill in the blanks about your new prospect.

When I get the receptionist, I'll say: "Hi, this is John Boyens, with the Boyens Group®. I'd like to send some information to your VP of sales, but I don't have a name. Can you give me the name, specific title, mailing address, and telephone number?" The purpose of your call is just to gather data—not to engage in a meeting, and it's the best way to build your pipeline.

ABOUT THAT $300,000 DEAL

This brings us back to one of our best success stories, the one about landing the $300,000 contract in less than two weeks. Here's how it went down:

Using the letter/cold-call approach process, I made it through to the executive assistant, who gave me her e-mail address so that I could re-send the letter I had sent to my desired contact.

Five minutes after I sent it to her, she called me right back and said that I needed to call her boss at 7:30 on Friday morning. She also told me, "I won't be here at that time, but I've printed out a copy of the letter for him and will leave it on his desk with a Post-it note. He needs to talk to you."

Just what I wanted to hear. So at 7:30 that Friday, I had my conversation with the decision maker, and it went very well. Keep in mind I had never met these people before. No warm introduction or referral.

During my conversation with the decision maker, I engaged him with a couple of questions based on the letter, and his answers validated what his business needs were. During the conversation, I also discovered that his company was close to signing a contract with a training company out of Atlanta.

Near the end of our conversation, he said, "Could you be available on a conference call on Monday morning so you can talk to my regional vice president and our people over in Europe?"

"Yes, I can."

I didn't care at that time who was going to be on that call—all that mattered was my knowing that there would be a call. The door had been kicked wide open. So on Monday morning we had the conference call. That Wednesday, they asked me to send a proposal to them.

On Friday, we were given verbal approval for the deal. It took me about a week to work out all the language with the legal department, and then they signed the $300,000 contract that less than two weeks earlier was going to be awarded to that Atlanta company.

—John Boyens

SUMMARY OF KEY POINTS
(Chapter 5)

- Often there is an obstacle between you and the key person to whom you wish to speak, and successful salespeople always know how to work their way through those "gatekeepers."

- The three steps to work your way through the gatekeeper starts with a well-crafted letter to your prospect, ending with a promise to follow up within ten business days.

- The three most common types of gatekeepers are voicemail, the executive assistant, and the receptionist, and each have their own unique characteristics and hot buttons.

- Great successes, even those of the $300,000-contract variety, sometimes await just on the other side of the gatekeeper.

6

Weaving a
Web of Influence

One major mistake salespeople can make is what I call a "single-point failure." That is, when they start working with a new prospect, or even an existing client, they tend to focus all their energies on establishing a business relationship with only one person. While it's good to work your way toward finding the right person with whom you want to do business, preferably the decision maker, making that one person your sole contact doesn't bode well for long-term success with that organization.

A salesperson's focus should be on identifying the *key players* within the prospect's or client's organization. By identifying key players, salespeople can avoid the "single-point failure." If salespeople focus on only one person or one relationship, they could be left out in the cold should that person suddenly get promoted or leave the organization. This departure will always put the salesperson at significant risk!

Let me share a personal story that everyone can relate to. In a past business life, I was vice president of sales for a Fortune 500 company. When I first took over, I created a Lost Business Report. Salespeople were asked to fill out a form explaining why they had lost a piece of business. I wasn't trying to beat up the salespeople but rather understand why we were losing 20 percent of our customer base each year! Interestingly enough, not once in the eighteen months of having salespeople complete this report did a salesperson ever write in the reason for losing a piece of business as being because they got outsold. The number-one reason given for losing business was "their contact had left the company." And to that I would say, "Well, did they take the whole building with them?" Of course they didn't!

A successful client relationship that is built for the long-term should involve establishing yourself with several people at different levels and in various functional roles within the organization. This is how you can weave a web of influence throughout an organization. We will be introducing specific tools such as Pyramid of Power, Problem Positioning Grid, and Solution Targeting Grid to help you weave your web.

◦━━◆━━◦

THE PYRAMID OF POWER

Knowing the pyramid of power within any organization allows you to recognize who the key people are in the company. It is necessary to know who is at the top of the pyramid (the Office of the "CxO"), which includes owners, presidents, and other C-level (CFO, COO, CEO, etc.) executives. It also means being familiar with the middle tier of the organization (Line of Business Executives) including all of the functional areas, such as sales, marketing, operations, finance, human resources, communications, etc. It is also important to know the staff executives. These are the people responsible for executing the day-to-day activities.

When you weave a web of influence, realize that there is never any one problem in a company that is strictly limited to one department. A problem or need affects the entire organization, and it's that salesperson's job to weave that web of influence throughout the entire company to get them to acknowledge the impact and agree to take action.

It's important to note that salespeople often get delegated to people whom they speak most like. Let me give you an example. Let's say that you sell a technology solution and that you're speaking with the president of one of your largest prospects. Let's say the president is not a technologist. If you start talking about the features or functions of your solution, odds are that he or she will delegate you to someone in the IT department because you didn't focus your conversation on the topics that are of interest to the president's position.

> *It's important to note that salespeople often get delegated to people whom they speak most like.*

❦

Pyramid of Power

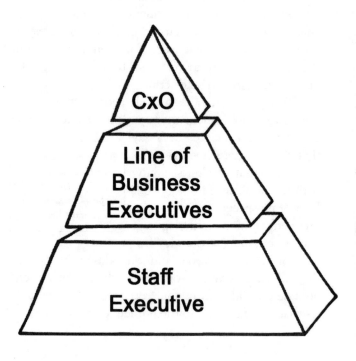

PROBLEM POSITIONING GRID

In business today everyone is tuned to radio station WIIFM! What's In It For Me?! In other words, all prospects have a set of buying criteria based on their position and job function.

The Problem Positioning Grid (PPG), pictured on the next page, will help you uncover the buying criteria by position and job function. Using the PPG during a sales call will help you focus your conversation on what's important to your audience.

Let me describe how to fill out the Problem Positioning Grid, which is illustrated on the next two pages. It has three columns:

- The first column highlights the job titles or functional areas that you are selling to.

- The middle column highlights responsibilities—not as it relates to your solution but rather what these people were hired to do, how they are measured, and what could cause them to get fired.

- The third column highlights specific company needs that could be addressed by your product or service.

Problem Positioning Grid		
Job Function	Responsibilities	What needs can your solutions address?

Let me give you an example of how to use the grid. Let's say you sell customer relationship management (CRM) software to the hospitality industry. Here are three titles you could sell to, and this is an example of what a completed grid would look like:

Job Function	Responsibilities	What needs can your solutions address?
CFO	• Establishing budget • Managing cash flow • Setting policies and procedures • Governmental reporting • Making profit	• Improving cash flow by increasing the number of room nights sold • Reduce costs by leveraging technology • Staying within budget
VP, Marketing	• Growing brand • Increasing market share • Establishing market messaging • Increasing occupancy	• Improve customer satisfaction • Increase market share • Better/more proactive communication with customers
VP, Customer Service	• Increasing customer satisfaction • Increasing return stays • Minimizing complaints • Resolving problems quickly	• Quickly resolve issues • Improve customer satisfaction • Improve operating efficiency

Once salespeople complete the Problem Positioning Grid, they are better able to align their product/service with their buyer's motivation. It helps salespeople understand their buyer and then speak to issues that benefit the buyer.

SOLUTION TARGETING GRID

People buy for their own, unique reasons. Successful salespeople use the Solution Targeting Grid to speak to each buyer individually and personally! The Solution Targeting Grid (STG), pictured on the next page, helps you delineate the value of your product/service to the benefit of your buyer. The STG includes three sections:

1. The Solution identifies a particular product or service you have to sell.

2. Job Function or Title highlights which job functions or titles could benefit from your product or service.

3. Positive Changes identifies how your product or service can make their job easier.

Both the Problem Positioning Grid and Solution Targeting Grid give detailed information on the buyer's incentive to buy, which in turn empowers the salesperson to target the prospects who are likely to purchase their solution. This gives the salespeople the confidence to make lots of calls because they know the value of their product/service to new customers.

Solution Targeting Grid

Solution _____

Job Function or Title	Positive Changes in their daily work activities
_____	_____
_____	_____
_____	_____

Solution _____

_____	_____
_____	_____
_____	_____

Solution _____

_____	_____
_____	_____
_____	_____

WEAVING THE WEB

Many years ago I was about to sign the biggest contract in the history of the company I was working for at the time. My contact at the prospect company, my sponsor so to speak, was the vice president of finance. The sole purpose of the meeting was to sign the contract and begin the integration of our services. Or so I thought.

We met in her office. After we exchanged pleasantries, she asked if the contract I had in my hand was the same as the one that a week earlier had been forwarded to her for her review and approval. After I told her it was, she said, "Everything looks great; I just need to get it approved upstairs."

Not only was I unaware that there was "an upstairs," I also didn't know who "lived" upstairs! My sponsor finally returned after forty-five minutes to state what by now was a foregone conclusion: "We have a problem." Looking back on this painful situation, I learned that she was asked two very important questions:

1. Who else have you looked at?

2. How do you know you're getting the best deal?

Because my sponsor had not taken other bids on the same service, she couldn't justify our price to the other executives. On top of that, while my sponsor was the ultimate decision maker (at least I had that part right), she still needed a second signature on the deal because it was for close to half a million dollars. It is not uncommon for many organizations to require two signatures for any purchase over a threshold figure, say, $25,000, and that figure gets even smaller at other companies. It is critical that salespeople are aware of the decision-making process and their sponsors' signature levels.

Fortunately, it was a salvageable deal, although it did take another forty-five days to win the business at 85 percent of the original contract amount.

Lessons learned:

• Even when the prospect assures you he or she is the decision maker, always be sure to ask, "Will yours be the only name on the contract?"

• Be absolutely sure to weave powerful webs of influence at your accounts and in your markets to increase the probability you can win the business and hold onto it through personnel changes.

• Leverage the power of the pyramid ("CxO," line of business executives, and staff executives) to learn who has "the power of the pen" and to maximize your opportunities within customer and prospect organizations.

• Engage multiple sponsors and/or influencers within the organization as a safety net should your primary sponsor move on.

—John Boyens

SUMMARY OF KEY POINTS
(Chapter 6)

- No one problem or need in a company or organization is strictly limited to one department.

- A salesperson's focus should be on identifying the key players within the prospect's or client's organization. By identifying key players, salespeople can avoid the "single-point failure."

- Salespeople need to be aware of the decision-making process as well as their sponsors' signature levels.

- Salespeople need to create Problem Positioning Grid and Solution Targeting Grid libraries to help weave their web of influence.

7

Have an IDEA Who You Are Selling To

People rarely buy products or services; they buy *solutions*. What exactly is a "solution"? The simple definition: an answer to a problem. An important selling tip is that if your prospect owns the problem, he or she must also take the action to solve their problem. You provide capabilities that enable the buyer to solve the problem. Top-performing salespeople are able to tailor their solutions to the unique needs of the individuals to whom they are selling.

> *People rarely buy products or services; they buy solutions.*

As I mentioned in the previous chapter, salespeople often get delegated to whom they speak most like. If you happen to break through right at the right level (top of the pyramid) but start talking about features and functions of your product or service, you will most likely get delegated lower in the pyramid to a level more suitable to the language you are using. *The best*

> *The best salespeople are the ones who speak the right language with the right level in the Pyramid of Power.*

63

salespeople are the ones who speak the right language with the right level in the Pyramid of Power.

☞━━☜

HAVE AN IDEA

Salespeople have to sell to all levels within an organization. The best salespeople always have an IDEA of who they are selling to. IDEA stands for:

I – Influencer. These people don't have decision-making power or signature authority, but they do have the ear of those folks in the organization who do have those powers.

D – Decision maker. They have the "power of the pen."

E – End user. This is the person or persons who will be hands-on using or implementing what is being sold, and they are going to want to know features and functionality of the product or service. They can't say "yes," but they can say "no."

A – Approver. This can be the person that the decision maker is often accountable to, and it's likely that this person will also be the required second signature on deals above a certain dollar threshold at the organization/company.

Naturally, in some organizations, people wear multiple hats, but normally one hat is primary. Once you discover which hat is that primary one, you will be able to stay in alignment with their specific needs. You will be able to speak their language.

In order to be successful, you must have an IDEA who you're selling to as well as how to sell to each of those four types of buyers. It's important to sell to each one differently. For example, you shouldn't reveal pricing or terms to end users (that kind of information is practically meaningless to them). That interaction should be saved exclusively for the decision maker. Conversely, your demonstration of the product or service should be made to the end user, not to the decision maker.

To sell effectively and consistently, salespeople must have done their homework (such as pre-call research on prospects, which we discussed earlier in the book).

◦━━✦━━◦

PRODUCT CAPABILITY KNOWLEDGE

To be successful in sales, it is very important to know what your product or service is, what it does, who would use it, and how it would benefit the user. This strategy is what we call "product capability knowledge" vs. simply "product knowledge." Salespeople should focus on what their prospect is buying versus what it is that they're selling.

> *Salespeople should focus on what their prospect is buying versus what it is that they're selling.*

Let's say, for example, that you sell an accounting software package that has an automated commission-reporting feature that can be sorted by customer, territory, and salesperson. How would this feature benefit the district sales manager? Perhaps it could help him or her compile monthly status reports more quickly. Or maybe it could help measure teams' performance. Perhaps it would enable the manager to realign sales territories.

Now turn it around and think about what bad things would happen if sales managers didn't buy your product. They could waste time and lose productivity if unable to compile their monthly reports in a timely fashion. Or, without the software, they could unwittingly increase administrative costs because they would have to track their teams' respective performances manually. Worse yet, they would be unable to realign their territories with automated tools, which in turn would cause current negative sales performance to continue.

How about the CFOs? What would this product mean to them? To start with, it could probably help close their books more quickly. It might also provide backup documentation and create audit trails. It might even enable them to improve their reporting on a monthly basis.

And what would be the consequences if they didn't have your product? Reports might be late or inaccurate. There might be cash flow problems. Manual processes could cause errors in projections.

Finally, let's discuss the president or owner. Your product could help increase customer satisfaction. Perhaps it would improve cash flow by getting bills paid faster.

Top-performing salespeople have a knack for being viewed as consultants by their clients and not as vendors pushing products. They are able to target their solution to the needs of their individual buyers because they understand the capabilities of their products.

SUMMARY OF KEY POINTS
(Chapter 7)

- You get delegated to whom you speak most like.

- People rarely buy products or services; they buy solutions.

- Have an IDEA who you are selling to (Influencer, Decision maker, End user, or Approver).

- Today's buyer expects you to be prepared and to have done your homework.

- Ensure product capability knowledge, which entails knowing what your product or service is, what it does, who would use it, and how it would benefit the user.

- Top-performing salespeople are viewed as consultants by their clients. They are able to target their solutions to the needs of their individual buyers.

8
Selling Value, Not Price

Have you ever lost a sale because you were told your price was too high? If you've been in sales for twenty minutes, it probably has happened to you three times already. Have you ever been told that you lost the sale because, "the value was too high!"?

—John Boyens

No surprise there. Today's successful salesperson recognizes price objections for what they really are—a bargaining tool for a customer who wants to be sure he or she is getting the best deal. The skill that salespeople must learn is to direct the conversation toward value, not price. *The best salespeople are able to uncover the customer's need, analyze the costs associated with that need, create a vision with a bias toward their capabilities, and then, and only then, unveil proof.*

> *The best salespeople are able to uncover the customer's need, analyze the costs associated with that need, create a vision with a bias toward their capabilities, and then, and only then, unveil proof.*

Many times, the customer who objects to the price is merely testing to be sure that the best possible price is on the table. Sometimes the prospect will interchange the words "price" and "cost." When that happens, it's important to recognize that there is a difference. *Price* is what a supplier charges for a product or service. *Cost* is calculated by adding the value to be received compared to the money being spent for the purchase.

⚬━✦━⚬

COST JUSTIFICATION

Our research shows that one of the primary reasons people don't buy is because they can't justify the cost of the investment or calculate a feasible payback. If salespeople quote prices before the customer has seen value, a price objection usually results. Those salespeople lost because they failed to translate their product features into capabilities that will empower the buyer.

> *Our research shows that one of the primary reasons people don't buy is because they can't justify the cost of the investment or calculate a feasible payback.*

The best time to establish value and build the cost justification necessary to close the sale is during the need-development phase of the sales cycle, when customers are revealing their problems and issues. By investing

Another Boyens Group® client, Hunter McCarty, COO of R. J. Young, has been involved in sales long enough to know all about selling value vs. price and the importance of letting the buyer know that shopping on price often could mean a high cost of doing business ultimately.

"One of the most important things in sales is to establish a solid value proposition," Hunter says. "People are interested in three things—quality, service, price. If you leave one out, that's the one that you will have to suffer with. Everybody wants all three, but let's say I ask a prospect to pick which two he wants and he says quality and service, then I tell him he's going to have to pay a higher price. He doesn't want to do that, either. That's a paradigm we are faced with every day."

time to discover the costs from the potential buyer, the perception of value will be established, thereby eliminating or at least diminishing objections when the price is revealed.

Here are two methods to use to establish value with the buyer:

1. Show your prospects how your product or service can help increase revenue.

2. Show your prospects how your product or service will reduce their costs of doing business.

    For instance:

    *   Can your product or service help your prospect eliminate an existing cost completely?

71

- Can your product or service help your prospect avoid paying future costs?

- Can your product or service help your prospect redirect an existing cost to make better use of an existing resource?

There are "soft costs" as well. For instance, can your product or service help improve their image or solidify their brand? One tool we introduce in the Productive Selling Zone® workshop that focuses on establishing value from the prospect's perspective is called VALU Builder©.

VALU Builder© has four steps:

1. Verify the business issues facing your prospects today.

2. Ask questions/analyze impact about how they do things today without your product/service.

3. Link your unique capabilities so they can see themselves using your product/service.

4. Unveil proof and unveil price.

VALU Builder©
enables the buyer to
buy. The fact is
that most people
don't like to be sold
. . . but everyone
likes to buy!

VALU Builder© enables the buyer to buy. The fact is that most people don't like to be sold . . . but everyone likes to buy! In order to stay in alignment with your buyer, use the outline on the following page to recap the information captured when completing your VALU Builder©. We call this outline a VALU Letter.

VALU Letter

Dear _____ :

I appreciate the opportunity we had to meet last (<u>day of the week</u>) and to discuss some of the current issues at (<u>name of prospect's company</u>). The purpose of this letter is to recap our meeting to ensure that I have captured the information correctly and to confirm our next steps.

Your most important business issue at this point is

_____

This is occurring due to

1. _____
2. _____
3. _____
4. _____

As a result, you are experiencing a substantial cost in

_____

In addition to your department, this issue is also creating an impact on _____

because _____

You are looking for a solution to provide you with the capability to _____

I believe that I can provide that capability and would like the opportunity to prove it to you. As a result, I have made arrangements to _____

I will call you on (<u>date</u>) to confirm.

Sincerely,

Another one of our clients, Mark Ward, a long-time sales executive, took the idea of a follow-up letter and has used it over and over to his advantage, as he explains:

"John's approach and framework to summarize a conversation with a potential buyer via a VALU Letter is very effective. It enables the seller to capture the highlights and confirm the next steps. By closing with a statement along the lines of 'If I have misrepresented the conversation, please feel free to clarify,' you gain further concurrence. These letters certainly decrease the sales process by offering clarity and a call to action."

SCIENCE TO SELLING

> *There is a science to selling, and it involves a fairly simple formula, which is: Need + Vision = Sale.*

Oftentimes salespeople believe that selling is more of an "art" rather than a "science." I beg to differ! There is a science to selling, and it involves a fairly simple formula, which is: **Need + Vision = Sale**. This means that if you are able to uncover a need, or if you're able to create a vision for a new way of doing something, you have a chance to make the sale. You've established value, and the objection to price won't even come up.

Conversely, if you don't uncover need or create a new vision, you could have the best product, the lowest price, and the greatest reputation, but that prospect is not going to buy. The "Need + Vision = Sale" (N+V=S) formula is the catalyst for creating a productive selling process that is both measurable and quantifiable.

<hr/>

ESTABLISHING VALUE

Value-added salespeople use their products or services to show customers the value they are getting compared to the money paid. They understand that value is determined by the buyer, so let me delineate the five keys to establishing value:

Five Keys to Establishing Value

1. Show how your product or service can help increase revenue.

2. Demonstrate how you can help prospects eliminate specific costs.

3. Identify how you can help prospects avoid paying future costs.

4. Show how prospects can redirect a present cost to make better use of an existing resource.

5. Understand how your product or service can help prospects improve their image or solidify their brand.

> *The best time to establish value and build the cost-justification necessary to close a sale is during the need-development phase of the sales cycle, which is when customers are revealing their problems and issues.*

The best time to establish value and build the cost-justification necessary to close a sale is during the need-development phase of the sales cycle, which is when customers are revealing their problems and issues. *By investing the time to discover the costs to the potential buyer, the perception of value will be established, eliminating objections when the price is revealed.*

○━━◆━━○

USING METRICS

One more thing to emphasize when it comes to value justification is that it's important to do more than just sell value—you must sell quantifiable value. Value needs to be shown in dollars, percentages, or numbers, period.

This gets back to your prospects' cost of doing business the old way, without your solution. In order to understand buyers' business issues, you must understand what it costs them to do business the way they are doing it today. And you need to be able to show them what those *undesirable* costs are.

Once you are able to communicate to buyers *your* capabilities and/or *your* solutions, you will be able to show them how you can help them lower their costs or increase their revenues or improve their operating efficiency. By using your product or service, the prospects could process one more loan application per day, or

76

gain one point of market share, or reduce their operating expenses by more than $10,000 per week.

There are two concepts in particular at work here benefiting the buyer once he does business with you: Return on Investment (ROI) and Internal Rate of Return (IRR). Don't assume your prospect is going to take the lead in figuring out how your product

> *When it comes to value justification, it's important to do more than just sell value—you must sell quantifiable value. Value needs to be shown in dollars, percentages, or numbers, period.*

or service will be beneficial in either one of those respects. It is up to the salesperson to have those numbers at the ready, painting a picture for the prospect in dollars and cents.

SUMMARY OF KEY POINTS
(Chapter 8)

- The best salespeople are able to uncover the customer's need, analyze the costs associated with that need, create a vision with a bias toward their capabilities, and then, and only then, unveil proof.

- Price objections are often a customer's bargaining tool to make sure they are getting the best deal.

- Customers reveal their problems and issues during the need phase of the sales cycle.

- Selling is a science that follows the formula of N+V=S (Need + Vision = Sale).

- Value-added salespeople use their products or services to show customers the value they are getting compared to the money being paid.

- Establishing value can minimize last-minute negotiations at the end of the sales cycle.

- Don't assume that your prospects will calculate ROI or IRR. It is up to the salesperson to walk them through the calculation to establish the value to be gained in lowering their costs, increasing their revenues or improving their operating efficiency.

9

Empowering Decision Makers

Too many salespeople engage in tactical kinds of conversation (e.g., responding to a Request For Proposal, reacting to a phone call, etc.) as opposed to engaging in strategic, proactive conversations with their prospects.

To empower decision makers, it is first important to know who they are. Identifying the key players should be one of the three main objectives a salesperson should have when placing an initial sales call to a new prospect. (Revisit the pre-call planning process mentioned in Chapter 4, "Pipeline Development." Also, in Chapter 6, "Weaving a Web of Influence," we touched on the subject of finding out who the decision maker is and what makes him or her "tick.")

To make sure you are speaking with someone who can buy, ask one of the following four questions. Remember, don't ask all four; just pick the one that you deem the best fit for a particular scenario:

1. "Among the people impacted, who can help us move forward on the project?"

2. "If we need to solicit support, who else will be involved in the buying decision?"

3. "What do you see as the next step and time frame?"

4. "Besides yourself, who else is involved in the final decision?"

Their response will let you know if you're at the right level in the Pyramid of Power (chapter 6).

⊶✦⊷

THE SO-WHAT? FUNNEL

During our workshops we introduce a concept called the "So What?" Funnel. The So-What? Funnel refers to how often the buyer is thinking "So What?" during a salesperson's presentation about the features and function of his or her product.

While buyers have hundreds of needs, salespeople should focus on four. Show the buyers how your product or service can help them *increase revenue, decrease costs, improve operating efficiency,* or *become compliant.* If you focus on anything else, chances are your prospect is thinking "So what?"

A visual of the So-What? Funnel is presented on the next page.

So-What? Funnel

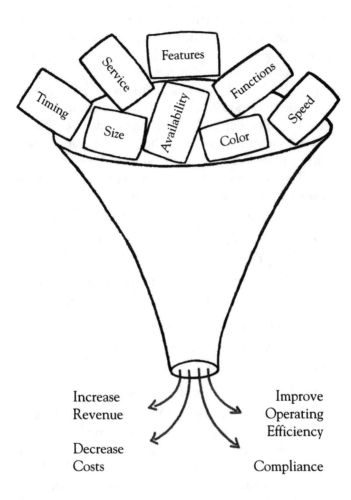

Working your way to the decision maker carries with it a degree of difficulty depending on who your initial point of contact is. If you start lower in the organization, you have to move up the chain, and that's a harder way to sell. It's preferable to start higher in the organization and allow yourself to get delegated down.

If you've done your homework and are able to share that information with the decision makers, then they will find value in what you have to say.

Here's a checklist of how to prepare for calling on the decision maker. Be prepared to:

- Provide a brief introduction about your company
- Share a Credibility WINdow© (at a decision maker's level, introduced in Chapter 11)
- Share critical data from previous calls (if any)
- Facilitate a BIO© (to be introduced in Chapter 11)
- Facilitate a VALU Builder©
- Explore organizational impact (weave the web)
- Determine authority to buy
- Clarify next steps and timelines

So, how do you engage? Your opening for the decision maker meeting can sound something like this:

"I appreciate the opportunity to meet with you today. In the time allowed, I thought it would be helpful to understand the business issues from your perspective and to update you on recent meetings with Fred and Sally. Then we can mutually decide how to proceed. Is there anything else you'd like to add?"

Make sure that you talk about mission-critical initiatives. Ask the decision maker to identify the top two initiatives on his or her plate, or to project the top two business challenges over the next six to twelve months. Use whatever verbiage is comfortable for you.

Once you've established your credibility and the buyer has given you some buying signals, then you are poised to consummate the sale. Here are some examples of buying signals, both verbal and nonverbal.

Verbal Communication

- "Can I get that in blue or black?" When they start asking you specific things about your product, that's a very good sign.

- "How long will it take to implement it?" The buyers are starting to figure out how they get to start using the product.

- "Do you accept credit cards?" They want to buy! Make it easy for them to do so.

Nonverbal Communication

- Leaning forward. If the person has been sitting back and all of a sudden leans forward when you say something, or picks up a pen, or makes a note—recognize you just hit something.

- Closing the collateral material and looking for a contract.

SUMMARY OF KEY POINTS
(Chapter 9)

- Salespeople spend too much time selling to people who can't buy.

- Learn who the key decision makers are and how they make key decisions.

- Make sure you show buyers how your product or service can help them increase revenue, decrease costs, improve operating efficiencies, or become compliant.

- Once you get to decision makers, you need to know how to engage them in discussion, focusing in on their mission-critical initiatives.

10
Getting the Buyer to Buy

> You've done all of the right things; you've performed all the levels of proof; you've met with all of the key people; and you've done the cost justification required. However, the prospect still will not pull the trigger and sign the contract. Isn't that a salesperson's worst nightmare?
>
> **—John Boyens**

People have a tendency to do things out of habit. That's true for buyers and sellers. Because of habit, buyers are averse to risk, including the risk of changing vendors or suppliers. Prospects will default to a concept called "status quo."

Let me tell you that there is no such thing as status quo! Businesses are either moving ahead or falling behind...but they certainly are not standing still! Competitive pressures, marketplace conditions, economic changes, employee turnover, changes in customers, and dependency on technology are just a few reasons why businesses aren't able to stand still.

So if you're having a difficult time getting your prospects to admit need, or if you're having a situation where your prospects keep delaying their decision, then it's time to figure out a way to give them a nudge. They don't seem to have the same sense of urgency that you do, and you don't know if they ever will.

All of us have been in those sales situations where we go through our checklist, and say and do everything we know we are supposed to do. We also know that our prospects are soaking it all up and starting to show some of the right buying behaviors and verbiage, but you still are not getting them over the hump.

Why aren't they buying?

Often the buyers' sticking point is the "fear" of change. You're asking them to change, but to them change is the great unknown.

There are four reasons why people fear change:

1. **Emotion**. The fear of the unknown, uncertainty, and mistrust.

2. **Perception**. They don't see the need for change. Maybe they are leaders in their industry, and their competitors are nipping at their heels, but they haven't felt the pain yet, so they don't see the need to change. By the time they recognize it, it's too late.

3. **Attitude**. They believe most changes are not for the better.

4. **Reluctance**. This is a wait-and-see attitude. They say, "Let's see what our competitors will do, and

then we'll step up to change." The most success-ful companies will address change long before they must.

⊙══✦══⊙

RISK IT

All this talk about creating a sense of urgency within buyers goes back to Chapter 1, where we talked about the reasons buyers don't buy and then segued into the three stages of buying. The third and final one, as you might remember, was the risk stage.

Buyers think to themselves, "What if it's not the right choice, what if it doesn't work, are we really get-ting the best deal, etc.?" There are three things you can do in the risk-assessment piece that allow you to mini-mize that challenge:

1. Talk about the financial impact. Review the cost of delay or the cost of no decision.

2. Talk about the successes to be gained.

3. Discuss the consequences. In other words, what bad things happen if they don't make the deci-sion to change? They will still have the same challenges as when you first engaged.

Again, point out to the prospects the cost of delay or the cost of no decision. You want them to under-stand the following facts:

*   Their business problem doesn't go away unless *they take action.*

*   The reason they took a meeting with you is because they had a business problem.

87

- Numbers don't lie! There are costs associated with their problem.

- Their problem is probably affecting other departments as well.

Bob Danser, business development manager with Goldleaf Financial, has found that creating a sense of urgency in a prospect is a tactic he needs to call on fairly frequently:

"I definitely have to interject some urgency into a number of my presentations. Our sale is a multi-step process. Typically, there is more than one principal in a company involved in the process, and it seems like there's always one who is slowing things down. In so many words I will ask, 'What are your other options, and what will you do if they don't succeed?' We call it need-gap tension."

CHANGE THE MESSAGE

If salespeople want to minimize the "fear" of change and help create a sense of urgency in buyers, they should use our four-step, change-message model.

1. **State the change.** One sentence.

2. **The payoffs.** Why do they need to make the change? Perhaps it's the pace of competition, or the marketplace. Or it could be their clients are asking them to change.

3. **Support.** You have to be able to articulate the transition strategy. How do you get them to switch from the supplier they've been doing business with for a long time to doing business with you? How do you make it easy to do business with you and make that transition relatively seamless?

4. **Be optimistic.** Be positive about the future. Restate the benefits that they are going to gain by making this change. These could include increased revenue, increased market share, better margins, etc.

Salespeople should articulate and help quantify the cost and the risk of having their prospects stay where they are. The bottom line is if your prospects do not *proactively* react to change, then they have to face it *reactively*, and that is no way to run a successful business.

SUMMARY OF KEY POINTS
(Chapter 10)

- Some prospects are creatures of habit who are averse to change; establishing value with those people usually isn't enough to get them to close.

- A good salesperson knows how to show reluctant buyers that it's *more painful* to keep doing things the way they are.

- Creating a sense of urgency in buyers requires wise use of numbers—specifically dollars—to get your selling point across.

- There are four primary reasons that people ignore change:
    1. Emotion
    2. Perception
    3. Attitude
    4. Reluctance

- Use our four-step, change-message model to empower the buyer to make a change. Create a sense of urgency for the buyer.

11

Uncovering Need

One of the most difficult tasks faced by salespeople is to get their prospect to admit need. In our workshops we introduce four tools to help uncover need. We've already discussed two of these in Chapter 6:

1. Problem Positioning Grid
2. Solution Targeting Grid

There are two other tools that I'd like to introduce: Credibility WINdow© and Business Interview Organizer (BIO©).

CREDIBILITY WINdow©

Credibility WINdow© is a four-step communication tool that allows you to uncover "need" by sharing a previous success story. The four steps include your introduction, reasons, goals, and outcome of your success story. If your prospects relate to your story, there's a good chance that they visualize a similar need.

Every company should build a library of Credibility WINdows© that will allow them to utilize past successes to "win" future business. It is important to note that any salesperson is able to use the Credibility

Credibility WINdow©

Introduction	**Reasons**
Match the former success scenario as closely as possible to your prospect's needs. Tell about a challenge your current customer (no specific names yet!) was having before your solution. "I was working with another (<u>similar job title</u>) who was having a challenge with . . ." 1 ——▶ 2	Describe specific reasons for the challenge that only your solution was able to address. "This customer was frustrated because . . . "
Goals 3 ——▶ 4	**Outcome**
Describe what your customer was hoping to be able to do with your solutions. "What this customer wanted to be able to do was . . . "	Describe any metrics the customer gained as a result of using your solution. "With our solution, this customer was able to achieve these results . . . "

WINdow© even if they were not the salesperson who made the sale. As long as the story is true, a salesperson is able to leverage the Credibility WINdow© as if it were their own. In fact, the salesperson's company provided products, services, or capabilities that enabled their client to solve specific business challenges.

Yankelovich Executive Vice President of Sales Kevin Brown offers an assessment that touches on aspects of the Credibility WINdow© and BIO©, among other things:

"John's approach when it comes to asking for the order is really a natural outcome of a tightly managed process all the way through the 'buy cycle.' It is important to have a base of knowledge about the prospect before the call; when available, reading their annual report, listening to the quarterly earnings call, using resource tools like Hoover's, etc... It provides an external view of the prospect's business and industry.

Credibility comes from what you know about the client initially, but more importantly from how you differentiate yourself by how you sell. That builds the most credibility. I think this is one of John's key messages. An example of this is BIO©. It is a great approach that allows us to get the prospect talking, to facilitate sharing of information that is painless for the prospect and incredibly valuable for the salesperson.

Every nuance of BIO© is important, for example, in helping the prospect communicate things that are working and things that are getting in the way. In less than four minutes, a salesperson will uncover the top two issues on the prospect's plate, which leads to a successful close."

BUSINESS INTERVIEW ORGANIZER (BIO©)

BIO© is a tool that engages the buyer in a sales conversation versus a sales presentation. It can be facilitated in person or over the phone and usually takes about four minutes.

BIO©
1. Start by getting prospects to talk about themselves and why they've been successful (e.g., name recognition, great products, competitive pricing, etc.). 2. Get them to acknowledge that all businesses have problems, things that get in the way of their success. 3. Next, you'll ask your prospects, "What's keeping you from being as successful as you'd like to be?" 4. Then, ask them, "If you could focus your attention on one or two items that would give you the biggest payback, what would they be?" 5. Lastly, ask your prospects, "Who is the person responsible for fixing the items that were identified?" You'll want to take notes to capture this important information throughout this process.

At the conclusion of a successful BIO©, you will have uncovered the following:

1. What is working well with your prospect today

2. What is getting in the way or keeping them from being as successful as they would like to be

3. The prioritization of the issues

4. The person responsible to take action

BIO©, Credibility WINdow©, and VALU Builder© are the foundational tools that facilitate sales effectiveness in a Productive Selling Zone®.

Bob Danser, business development manager of Goldleaf Financial, saw almost-immediate results once he learned what BIO© was:

"It was the day after four days of meetings in Nashville, which included two days with the folks from Boyens Group. One of the things I learned from John was BIO©, which really puts things in perspective and provides a structure for getting into a conversation with clients to find out where they are really at.

I had done things like this before, but never as concise as BIO©. My first presentation after learning about BIO© went just as advertised. Where most sales training looks at how things are done in a perfect world, BIO© deals with the real world.

In this case, it was my first meeting with the owner of a company, and using BIO© I was able to chart things out right in front of him. I asked him to go over things that had been successes for him as well as the challenges he was faced with.

In this case, it made a positive impact, and I was able to get a commitment from him right on the spot!"

RADIO STATION WIIFM

Let's revisit one of our concepts at work from our workshops, and that is "radio station" WIIFM. We discussed this concept earlier in the book when we introduced the Problem Positioning Grid. WIIFM stands for What's In It For Me?

The "me" in that, of course, actually refers to the prospect who is looking out for his or her own interests, in this case what there is to gain by going with your product or service. Early in the process, the prospect is wondering whether to continue this conversation or not.

Whenever a salesperson makes a call, he or she has to understand *why* the buyer is interested. If you as a salesperson can get focused in on what your buyer's *real* needs are, then there's a better chance you can engage them in such a way that they will at least take a serious look at your product or service.

Lastly, salespeople should ask a lot of situational and behavioral questions. Ask, "When this happens, what do you do?" or "When this occurs, how do you address that?" If you spend enough time asking relevant questions, you can learn a lot more about their specific business issues.

SUMMARY OF KEY POINTS
(Chapter 11)

- The Problem Positioning Grid, Solution Targeting Grid, Credibility WINdow©, and BIO© are four tools to help salespeople uncover need.

- The more business issues you identify that can link to your product or service, the easier it is to sell.

- Build a library of Credibility WINdows© to uncover "need" by sharing previous success stories with your prospects.

- Use BIO© to prioritize need from the *prospect's perspective*.

- BIO©, Credibility WINdow© and VALU Builder© are the foundational tools that facilitate sales effectiveness in a Productive Selling Zone®.

- Salespeople should ask a lot of situational and behavioral questions to learn more about their prospects' specific business issues.

12

The Secrets
of Master Negotiators

TRAITS OF THE BEST NEGOTIATORS

Establishing value with the buyer alone does not close the deal. A salesperson also needs to be prepared to negotiate in order to close the sale. Following are some traits of the best negotiators:

- They regard negotiation as an ongoing part of the selling process, not as a final event needed to close the sale.

- They know that the degree of their power is directly proportional to the amount and type of information they know about the buyer, and in this instance, knowledge truly is power.

- They actually listen, ask open-ended questions, and use silence as a strategic advantage.

- They give a little at a time . . . reluctantly and slowly.

- They never let negotiations get down to one item.

- Their demeanor is one of confidence and assurance (even when they feel neither inside).

- They are fully prepared for customer objections because they have analyzed all the variables that influence the customer's decisions in their pre-call planning.

—**John Boyens**

In order to be successful in sales, master negotiators *must* have a plan. Winging it is never a good option. A good negotiation plan is a prerequisite, and it should include team members across various functions within your organization, so it's not just the salesperson out there on his or her own island. You've heard the saying, "No man is an island"? The same holds true for a sales professional as well as professional sales teams. Here's a six-point plan to use when establishing your negotiation plan:

Establishing Your Negotiation Plan

1. Establish a negotiation team and roles. (Be sure to include cross-functional players from your organization.)

2. Identify "walk-away" points" (deal breakers).

3. Identify those areas in which you have flexibility (what you might give away in negotiations, if needed).

4. Keep the terms and conditions separate from the legal content. (In other words, don't have legal negotiate the terms and conditions.)

5. Establish a negotiation process.

6. Establish a negotiation timetable.

What internal teams should you include in your negotiations? Finance, for one; bring them in to your plan so that everyone, including you, can understand the ripple effect across the board should you have to deviate on price prior to closing. Marketing should be involved if there are new products that are going to have to be developed to meet an unforeseen need (which we also like to refer to as "an opportunity").

The master negotiator also wants to identify and commit to walk-away points. These are the deal breakers, the predetermined points in the sales process which the salesperson can not cross without compromising the integrity of the sale. Likewise, it is good to be able to project what the prospect's own walk-away points will be. This kind of three-dimensional thinking will go a long way toward helping you to set some guidelines that serve as handy parameters. Walking away from a negotiation will be discussed in more detail later in the book.

THE CHARACTERISTICS OF NEGOTIATION

The best negotiators begin their negotiations as soon as they make first contact with a prospect. Maybe it starts over the phone when you try to make an initial appointment and suggest a day and time, but the prospect comes right back with a request to make it a different day and time. You now are in negotiations whether you like it or not!

Here are four characteristics of negotiations:

1. **Vendor normalization.** This is what buyers try to do—commoditize every product. Basically, they try to make every brand of product the equal of every other brand, including yours, so that they can focus in on negotiating price. If they get you to that point, you lose.

2. **Satisfy needs over wants.** Your job is to differentiate one from the other, and it might mean going against the grain of what the prospects think they want. Our job is to understand what they need. BIO© is a great tool to help identify needs in a priority fashion.

3. **Never panic or lose your composure.** It's okay to care about what you are doing and what you are selling, but don't become so desperate that you "lose it" when things start going sideways. Any salesperson is especially vulnerable to panicking if there is one more sale needed to make the monthly or their quarterly quota, but succumbing to panic will kill your negotiating ability.

4.   **Getting the approval you need!** We've already mentioned influencers, end users, and approvers, but what about beneficiaries, legal, technical, and administrative review? What about financial justification? Master negotiators know and accept all this going in, realizing they have ample opportunities in front of them to fully exercise their best persuasion tactics.

All this gets compressed when dealing with smaller sales and smaller companies, but if you are dealing with a Fortune 1000 company, the buyers have their own team to deal with, and you get to deal with them, too!

⚬══╾══⚬

BUYING TACTICS

You have the advantage in the negotiation process if you are able to get into the shoes of your buyer, to know where they are coming from so that you can be better prepared to anticipate their negotiating ploys.

A number of years ago, I got the chance to address the National Purchasing Managers Association meeting, and it was an interesting experience for me. The speaker immediately ahead of me was teaching the audience how to be better buyers. This, I thought, I needed to hear. It gave me an inside look at what "the guys on the other side" are doing during their negotiations with salespeople, and there are some good lessons to be learned here.

Again, remember that she was speaking from the point of view of the buyer—your prospect:

- Never sole source. Never get locked in to one vendor; otherwise, you won't be able to beat them up on price or terms (and you thought you were just being paranoid in those instances).

- Negotiate what you want in reverse preference order—that is, from lowest priority to top. Don't ask for the big concession upfront; rather, look for little concessions along the way, saving the big one for the end.

- Create supplier managers—somebody who will call salespeople back and get them in the loop and make them think they are winning even if they are not, so as to create conflict between salespeople to get the best price, the best terms, the best deal.

- Take it away from them at least once. Skilled buyers will try and delay the purchase to see if the salesperson will "sweeten" the deal.

HANDLING THE RISK PHASE

Remember that there are three phases of buying: need, proof, and risk. Here are some guidelines on how to handle the risk phase:

- Acknowledge the buyer's concern. Don't discredit, diminish, or dismiss it. It might not be a big issue to you, but *their perception is your reality*.

- Address their concern if you have the credibility to do so. If you don't have the credibility to do so, find someone in your organization who does.

- Focus on the original issues, the problems, and the costs the organization was having before engaging you. Their problems will not go away unless they take action with you and buy from you.

- Project the future impact. If they don't step up to address these issues, how is that going to impact them going forward?

- Acknowledge the importance of the decision.

- Encourage them to proceed.

Remember—don't answer questions that were never asked. If somebody says to you at the end of the buy cycle, "Boy, that's a lot of money," recognize that there isn't a question mark at the end of that sentence. Unfortunately, most salespeople will respond to that sentence as if it were actually a question, and they end up negotiating against themselves.

IMPROVING NEGOTIATING SKILLS

Here are some negotiation tips:

TIP: Know that there are two emotional obstacles—one each for the buyer and seller—that must be crossed before an agreement is reached.

DETAIL: The buyer wants to make sure he is getting the best *deal* (as opposed to the best *price*). For the seller, the big obstacle is the inability to walk away if the deal isn't right.

TIP: The more knowledge you have about your prospect, the more negotiating power you will have.

105

Mark Ward, one of our clients introduced earlier, offers some of his own insights on negotiation:

"John reinforced with my team the concept of quid pro quo, on how you should only give to get.

While at Acxiom, we were working on a major multi-year deal with one of the nation's leading telecommunications long-distance providers. We had carefully planned our negotiating strategy and our walk-away position. At each point in the negotiations, we were able to secure something in return for giving up discount or services concession, and, as John taught us, we gave less each time.

We were at the final conversation and made our final statement, that this was a "fair" deal. The client wanted to think about it overnight. To the astonishment of my boss, I informed him that we were walking away, if necessary, in the morning. His response was, 'Are you crazy?!'

The next day, we were awarded the deal without giving another penny or ounce of blood!"

DETAIL: Start by figuring out what it costs your prospects to do business without your product or service today. Also, you can help your prospects calculate a return on their investments as well as the cost of a delayed decision because you will know the issues that they are facing.

TIP: Actively listen and ask open-ended questions.

DETAIL: Utilize situational and behavioral questions. For instance: "How do you identify and acquire new customers today?"

106

TIP: Keep an open mind, and don't make assumptions.

DETAIL: Treat every customer as unique. Start by asking questions to find out how—not if—their needs differ from those of competitors.

TIP: Exude confidence and assurance—even if you don't feel those things.

DETAIL: Don't let buyers see you sweat! They have to know that you are willing to walk away.

TIP: Give a little at a time, reluctantly and slowly.

DETAIL: Don't automatically drop your price when asked. Let the buyer make the first move on concessions before you make yours. If a lower price is requested, ask for a longer contract or a higher-volume buy.

TIP: Never let negotiations get down to just one item.

DETAIL: This is where you end up with a loser and a winner, when what you really want is a win-win.

TIP: Manage information skillfully.

DETAIL: Sometimes in an effort to show our breadth of experience and our knowledge, we tell the prospect everything we know at the very first meeting.

TIP: Set high expectations.

DETAIL: Expect to close the business. That belief will prepare you for a successful negotiation.

We all have our pressure points, which reminds me of a situation I went through in a previous business life. I was promoted to a district manager's position for the eleven Western states and had about thirty people on my team ranging from customer service and marketing people to technical support people, along with salespeople and two other managers.

Two weeks into the job, I called everybody into the conference room to inform the team that out of nine districts, ours had been ranked last in the previous sales period. While this was a perfect place for me to enjoy my first field-management position (I had no place to go but up), I had a lot of work to do. First on my list was to knock down a major obstacle.

No one in the history of this district had ever sold a deal greater than $100,000. So I put into place a two-day training program, for **everyone**, that would challenge them to make six-figure deals a reasonable course of business, not some pie-in-the-sky figure.

At the end of this two-day training program, I had all district employees (even those in non-sales positions) take turns standing in front of their peers for some role playing. In front of the room, looking their "classmates" in the eye as though they were a collective prospect negotiating a deal, each person had to say, "Based upon the work that has led us to this point and based upon the assessment we've done, I believe that we can help you, and the investment required to move forward is $100,000."

After the role plays, my team looked at me like I had three heads, because many of them were people whose roles had nothing to do with closing deals or selling contracts, but it made no difference—everyone had to do it, and they were videotaped in the process so that they could benefit from viewing their own presentation practice.

Guess what? One full year after I put those people through that "torturous" exercise, we had shot from last place to District of the Year for our company. We sold three contracts in excess of $100,000, including one for $582,000 to a very large financial services company in San Francisco.

—**John Boyens**

PREPARE TO "STAND FIRM"

Standing firm is a preconceived strategy of knowing exactly how you will handle specific objections before you hear them spoken to you. Be thorough in your preparation, anticipating objections to your product or service, so that you won't be caught off-guard when a prospect hits you with them. It's like being in the courtroom: a good attorney never asks a question without first knowing what the answer is likely to be.

> *Don't forget to include Cost Justification in all negotiations. You, as a salesperson, have to believe in the product or service you are selling. If you wouldn't buy it, then it's going to be really hard for you to sell it.*

Also have a minimum of two "push backs" at the ready. These will allow you to withstand the pressure exerted by the prospect to drop the price. Good salespeople know that while dropping the price seems like the easy way out, it is not the way to start a profitable, long-term customer relationship.

Pushback One should reinforce the successes the customer will gain by purchasing your product or service. Some examples of successes:

- Gain market share

- Increase revenue

- Shorten the time to market

- Ensure a successful product rollout

If the buyer is still adamant about the need to reduce price, then proceed to Pushback Two.

Pushback Two should reinforce the consequences of delaying the purchase of your product or service, such as:

- Costs continue to rise
- Sales targets could be missed
- Market share might be lost
- Employee turnover could increase

It's also a good idea to include "gives" and "gets" in your "Stand Firm" strategy when negotiating. A "give" could be free shipping, or special terms. A "get" could include items such as longer-term contracts or exclusives for certain products. It's not a good idea to offer up a "give" until the customer commits to one of your "gets." Be willing to give, but when you do, work it such that you will, in return, receive.

Don't forget to include Cost Justification in all negotiations. *You, as a salesperson, have to believe in the product or service you are selling. If you wouldn't buy it, then it's going to be really hard for you to sell it.*

SUMMARY OF KEY POINTS
(Chapter 12)

- Always be prepared to negotiate.

- Master negotiators regard negotiation as an ongoing part of the selling process, not as just a final event needed to close the sale.

- A good negotiation plan should include team members across various functions and not just a salesperson out there going solo.

- Establish firm walk-away points before the actual negotiation, not during.

- The best negotiators start their negotiations as soon as they make first contact with a prospect, and they emphasize needs over wants.

- Be prepared for the inevitability of dealing with savvy prospects who know as much about the negotiating process as you do— maybe they've even read this chapter, and your ability to remain cool in those situations with your wits about you will serve you well.

- Prepare to "Stand Firm" using cost justification.

13
Addressing Objections

- "It's too expensive."

- "I don't have the budget."

- "I've got to think about it."

- "It's not what we're looking for right now."

- "I need to shop around before I make a decision."

- "Why don't you send me a proposal, and I'll look it over and get back to you."

- "I want to talk it over with my partners."

I'm sure that you've heard these objections during your sales career! Objections are present in almost all negotiations, and there's no foolproof way of preventing them from being stated. You can do all the research you want on clients, get them to articulate their needs, create a vision, quantify the benefits of your product or service, establish credibility, and explain everything to them in any kind of language suitable to their position within the organization, and you still can get those little objections coming at you

> The best salespeople realize that they don't have to overcome objections but, rather, acknowledge and address them.

like mosquitoes in the woods right after a downpour.

The best salespeople realize that they don't have to overcome objections, but rather, acknowledge and address them.

DON'T BE AN OVERCOMER

The old school of sales insists that if a salesperson can just keep overcoming one objection after another, each step becomes just another trial close that will automatically lead to a sale once the prospect runs out of objections. I don't agree!

The most successful salespeople tweak their perspective, and instead of seeing sales as a process that includes *overcoming* objections, they see it as a process that involves *addressing* objections. There is a difference: The former opens things up to where the salesperson will say almost anything short of lying just to go around the objection, to move beyond it as just another hurdle to be cleared in the race to the finish line.

> The most successful salespeople tweak their perspective, and instead of seeing sales as a process that includes overcoming objections, they see it as a process that involves addressing objections.

The latter sees objections as an opportunity to reassure prospects by reminding them of needs or problems *they* already admitted relative to the particular objection. This requires a salesperson not only to be well prepared by knowing the prospect's needs and problems as well as or better than he does, but also to be a terrific listener, able to recall important information that has been discussed in the past.

> *Instead of thinking about overcoming objections, think about using your prospect's own information against his or her objection.*

Instead of thinking about *overcoming* objections, think about using your prospect's own information against his or her objection. That's not to suggest that you become contrary or combative in handling an objection—it means simply reminding the prospect of a key point or points that were made in an earlier conversation.

A sample exchange might go something like this:

PROSPECT: "All things considered, what you're offering me is just too expensive. We can't afford it."

SALESPERSON: "I'm not sure why you would say that. During our conversation, you acknowledged that your current marketing program is ineffective and is costing you $100,000 a quarter. The cost of our program is less than $35,000 in total and addresses the very root causes of the marketing problems that you identified. In fact, our program will pay for itself in three months. Just looking at the facts and figures as you explained to me earlier, it appears you can't afford to *not* make this change."

To minimize objections, the best salespeople do the following:

- Sell value, not price
- Find the real business issues for their buyer

115

- Understand how this buyer buys

- Know what they're up against as they relate to the competition and the marketplace

- Weave a web of influence across the company to which they are selling

- Create a sense of urgency with the buyer

- Empower decision makers to take action

TAKE NOTES

Another way to address objections is to be a good listener. There will be times that you will have to retrieve information on the spot about the prospect and his company in order to be able to handle an objection effectively.

Taking notes is the right thing to do. Never be shy about pulling out a notepad and pen or pencil to jot key points as they're discussed. Many of us fail to do a good job of taking notes. If we don't take good notes, we will be unable to recapture the information that was exchanged. It will also cause us to draw blanks when those objections start flying.

If you're not already doing it, get into the habit of grabbing a pad and pen every time you make or get a phone call or go out on a call. Then you can be ready to address any objections.

MANAGING THE SALES PROCESS

There are two tools that we introduce in our work-shops that help salespeople capture information useful to them throughout the sales process, including those moments that they encounter objections. One is the BIO© (Business Interview Organizer, introduced in Chapter 11), which is a tool we use to uncover a prospect's needs in a priority fashion, and the other is VALU Builder© (introduced in Chapter 8) which helps salespeople manage the sales process.

An important point to keep in mind is that being confronted with objections, as well as *addressing* objections, is not some sort of peripheral event or action separate from the rest of the sales process. Both are an integral, certainly not unexpected, part of what transpires during a negotiation, and the information used when "attacking" objections is the same information that is gathered during other parts of the sales process. Perhaps one aspect of objections that does set them apart from other elements of the process is that they can come without warning. *But instead of being shocked or dismayed by objections, the savvy salesperson will see them as opportunities to reinforce earlier selling points that need to be reviewed.*

> *Instead of being shocked or dismayed by objections, the savvy salesperson will see them as opportunities to reinforce earlier selling points that need to be reviewed.*

Let's take a closer, albeit brief, look at how BIO© and VALU Builder© can help salespeople address objections.

1. BIO© helps the salesperson learn more about the hows and whys of the way the prospect currently does business. The more information we can acquire about the prospect and his organization, the better we are able to see his needs, the way he buys, and where he is feeling the most pain. The avoidance of pain causes action. With all that in hand, we are then better qualified to address objections. Think of it this way: selling your product or service is not all about explaining it and showing off features; it's all about helping the buyer solve business issues or fill a need.

2. VALU Builder© enables salespeople to focus in on the most important business issues facing their prospect. It gives salespeople a guide to the sales process, keeping them on track to gather and analyze key information about their prospect. Key information could include:

- What it costs their prospect to do business without their products or services
- Competitive differentiation
- Cost justification
- Financial impact
- Organizational impact
- What you will need to do to "prove" your capabilities

Please note: Salespeople should *never* unveil price unless the prospect agrees to buy if satisfied with the proof given.

118

Once you gather information from BIO©, VALU Builder©, etc., you should be able to address any objection that comes your way.

◦═✦═◦

COST JUSTIFICATION

It's important to make sure the prospect understands that what you are offering is a good deal. You need to believe it as well; otherwise, it will be hard, if not impossible, to sell it.

One way to understand that it's a good deal is to use our Cost Justification worksheet, an example of which is shown on the next page. This is an internal document to convince yourself that what you're selling is a good deal.

Here's how it works:

In the top section, detail what the buyers will gain by purchasing your product; for instance, more revenue, cost savings, etc. Annualize the amount.

In the bottom section, detail what you're asking them to spend; for instance, hardware, software, etc. Annualize those costs.

When you subtract what you're asking them to spend from what they will gain, you can clearly see if it's a good deal or not. For your review, I've created a sample Cost Justification worksheet for a salesperson who sells marketing services.

Cost Justification Worksheet

When will the investment pay for itself?

What will be gained:

1.	Increased response rate by 1%	$250,000
2.	Decrease in undeliverable mail	$90,000
3.	More sales	$1,000,000
	Total Benefits/Savings	$1,340,000

What will be spent:

1.	Data license	$250,000
2.	Software	$125,000
3.	Analytics	$125,000
	Total costs	($500,000)

Total Net Benefits	$840,000

Cost of delay or nondecision $70,000/month
(Must have for an effective close!)

SUMMARY OF KEY POINTS
(Chapter 13)

- A potential buyer's objections are an inevitable part of the sales negotiation.

- The most successful salespeople look at objections as something to be *addressed*, not *overcome*.

- In addressing objections, you are actually using the prospect's own information "against" his or her objection.

- If we don't take good notes, we are unable to recapture the information that was exchanged, and that really hurts us when we have to address objections.

- If salespeople wouldn't buy what they're selling, their prospects won't buy either!

- It's important to make sure the prospect understands that what you are offering is a good deal. One way to delineate that for the buyer is to use our Cost Justification worksheet.

14
Knowing When
to Walk Away

I n my thirty-plus years of sales and sales management, I've never had a difficult prospect become a delightful customer! If they were difficult to deal with during the prospecting stage, they will likely be difficult to deal with from a customer service, billing, and customer-satisfaction perspective.

This was briefly touched on earlier, but it is worth further exploration.

There are two emotional hurdles that have to be cleared any time a sale is to take place. One hurdle is on the buyer's side, and one hurdle is on the seller's side:

- On the buyer's side, he or she has to figure it out: **"Am I getting a good *deal* or not?"** The issue here is not the lowest price, but the *best deal*, and deep down that is what the buyer is most concerned with.

- On the seller's side, the question salespeople should ask themselves (and it truly is a question that does have a correct answer), is, **"Am I willing to walk away?"** The correct answer is, of course, yes. Your first clue that you might be headed toward a "walk-away" scenario is when you discern one or more of the following:

  1. They're asking for too many concessions on our part.

  2. Their requested delivery time is just not realistic.

  3. As the deal stands now, we won't be able to make our normal profit margins.

  4. They're only going to buy this from us once, and then that will be the end of our relationship.

  5. They're making this a 'win/lose' scenario, and I'm losing!

  6. Their current vendor would never do that!

HAPPY EARS

We as salespeople tend to have "happy ears." That means we hear only what we want to hear, which nine times out of ten is that coveted proclamation from the buyer that they are now ready to sign the purchase order. Perhaps you were called in on the deal by the buyer in the twenty-third hour. There you are, one week away from closing the quarter, and you're hoping for that one deal that will *make that quarter* for you.

There are a number of warning signs that tell salespeople it's time to cut and walk away, but they don't always listen. Some of these warning signs include:

- The prospect doesn't actually fit your target customer profile

- The margins don't meet your requirements

- The deal would require a lot of customization

- The prospect won't give a commitment to future business or future orders

- The prospect won't grant you access to the decision maker

- The prospect has unreasonable timelines for delivery

- The prospect is making unreasonable demands in terms of time frame, colors, etc.

There are other warning signs, but those are some of the most common.

LISTEN YOUR WAY TO BETTER SALES

Sometimes in our eagerness to make the sale or close the deal, we forget to listen. Perhaps we forget to hear our prospects' needs or why they might be resistant to purchase our product or service. It's even conceivable that had you listened better earlier in the sales process, you would end up closing more deals satisfactorily and minimizing the number of times you end up having to walk away from the sale.

125

Here are six keys to *listen your way to better sales*:

1. Always bring a notepad to every meeting. Don't rely on scraps of paper to be scrounged up at the last minute.

2. Always take notes each time you speak with a prospect. Don't try to scribble down every word—jot down the key points. Key words or phrases usually are spoken with added emphasis, and they help uncover needs that only your product or service can satisfy.

3. Do your homework before making a call or going on an appointment to know what potential problems your prospect might be facing. This will enable you to pick up clues by practicing "active listening."

4. Paraphrase what you heard. This lets your prospects know that you understand what is being said, that you are not merely "parroting" back what has been said.

5. Mirror back your customers' sense of the facts, their evaluations, and what they desire and expect.

6. Know that sometimes when customers ask questions, they are just thinking out loud. It might be rhetorical in the sense they don't expect a response or solution from you, so give them the opportunity to work through their thoughts.

Our research has shown that customers react positively to these specific listening techniques, which is why the best salespeople use them on a consistent basis.

In addition, people retain only 10 percent of what they hear seventy-two hours after the fact, according to the book *Psychology of Memory*. Taking notes can increase your retention by another 20 percent.

Taking detailed notes also allows you to recap the important points of your conversation back to your prospect in a VALU Letter or VALU E-mail. It's a great way to create and maintain buyer-seller alignment. If you don't have buyer-seller alignment, you don't have a sale, and it's time to walk away!

SUMMARY OF KEY POINTS
(Chapter 14)

- There are two emotional hurdles that must be cleared any time a sale is to take place. One of those hurdles is on the buyer's side, "Am I getting the best *deal*?" and one is on the seller's side, "Am I willing to walk away?"

- Salespeople often tend to have "happy ears," hearing only what they want to hear.

- Be aware of warning signs that it might be time to walk away from a deal.

- Difficult prospects become difficult customers!

- Good listening skills include keeping a notepad handy and using it anytime you are in discussion with a prospect. Don't rely on your memory; it's not that good. Write it down!

- Taking notes enables your eyes and ears to work in harmony, which improves your ability to comprehend and retain what is being said. It also gives you the salient points of your conversation to compose a recap letter or to e-mail back to the prospect.

128

15

Asking for
the Order

Having a grasp of the building blocks of the sales process, such as targeting prospects, developing the pipeline, establishing credibility, weaving a web of influence, empowering decision makers, and addressing objections, have very little effect if you aren't *asking for the order*.

The trick is to ask for the order without *sounding* like you're asking for it. Done correctly, asking for the order is an ongoing process from start to finish.

Ultimately, our core mission as salespeople is not to dazzle prospects with product knowledge or do all the talking while they do all the listening. Salespeople are charged with closing orders and maintaining long-term relationships with their customers. To close business, you have to ask for it. I'm constantly amazed how many salespeople focus on their presentation or their proof, yet never actually ask for the order!

TEN SUREFIRE WAYS TO KILL A SALE

Here is a list of ten surefire ways to kill a sale before you ever get the chance to ask for it. These are the behaviors that leave you scratching your head and asking, "What happened? How did things go from so right to so wrong so quickly?"

1. *Prospect aimlessly. Grab anyone who will listen and give them the same sales pitch over and over again.*

2. *Be oblivious to the prospect's buying rhythm. Just jump in and sell.*

3. *Lead with as many features of your product or service as possible, with the idea that something is bound to stick.*

4. *Sell as low in the organization as possible. Don't bother with the decision makers (let alone trying to gain access to them).*

5. *Try to sell to someone who can't buy.*

6. *Make sure that your demos cover every aspect of every feature . . . or at least until your prospect falls asleep.*

7. *Badmouth the competition.*

8. *Miss deadlines or break promises.*

9. *Discount your price early and often.*

10. *Never differentiate yourself from your competition: after all, we're all the same, aren't we?*

GET THEM TALKING ABOUT THEMSELVES

People love to talk about themselves. This is especially true when it comes to answering questions posed to them by somebody who really seems to care. That's the role of the salesperson.

After you have established credibility (using past successes to leverage for your future successes with the Credibility WINdow©), you then get the prospect to start talking about his company. Ask one or more of the following questions:

- "Why does someone buy from them versus the competition?"

- "How do they differentiate themselves from their competition?"

- "What business issues are they facing?"

- "What are some of the reasons behind those issues?"

- "What major initiatives do they have going on at their company over the next twelve months?"

From there, it's a matter of getting into the details of those issues and then quantifying them. As mentioned earlier in this book, it's important to measure the results. For example, if you can show your prospect how you can help increase productivity by 15 percent, aren't you subliminally telling him or her to buy from *you* in order to get the measured results you just illustrated?

A good Credibility WINdow© will get people to start talking, asking questions such as:

- "How did you do that?"
- "Who did you do that for?"
- "How could it help me?"

All those questions are buying signs. If, however, you're having a difficult time getting your prospects to admit need, then you need to create a sense of urgency in them. (See Chapter 10.) Their reluctance to admit need relates to the fact that the fear of change is greater for them than the fear of staying where they are.

BUILDING CREDIBILITY

There's more to the notion of credibility than just success stories and testimonials. Salespeople must build credibility in the eyes of a prospect. Here are some ways you can build your own credibility with your prospects.

- You must believe that you offer value.
- Be willing to speak the truth.
- Have an attitude of win-win or no deal.
- Focus on the needs of the buyer, not on the needs of the seller.
- Solve problems rather than push products.
- Offer products or services once the buyer's needs are developed, not in advance of the needs.
- Be prepared to converse, not present.
- Address, not overcome, objections.
- Avoid high-pressure closings.

132

- Eliminate seller-oriented language, such as "pitch," "done deal," or "bag the big one."

Remember, buyers must feel good about the entire sales process, and it starts with their feeling good about you. Know this: Regardless of which stage of the sales process you are in, they are always asking themselves, "Is this the kind of person I would like to do business with?"

BECOME A CONSULTANT OR TRUSTED ADVISOR

On the subject of personal credibility, think of yourself as being a sales consultant or a trusted advisor. The best sales consultants:

- Establish a level of trust beyond the quality of the product or service itself.

- See themselves as problem solvers, and they expect to solve problems to help the customers achieve their goals.

- Recognize that they must have expertise; they need to be an authority in their field.

- Become strategic, and they focus on the customer's priorities and needs.

- Never stop asking questions.

- Believe in their company, their product or service, and they absolutely believe in themselves.

- Expect success, and they develop a high level of mental fitness.

133

To build credibility, use your past successes to generate future successes. Create an entire library of customer success stories; share some of the things you helped other clients do in achieving their business goals. Think about the problems those buyers had before they purchased your solutions. Also, think about the reasons they had those problems, and think about what their vision was for overcoming those problems. Most importantly, measure. Exactly how did your solution help them overcome their problems?

If you do all those things, you will build credibility with your clients now and in the future. In our thirty years of working with salespeople and sales managers, we have found that the best of the best already use some type of process to establish credibility. This brings us back to the concept of the Credibility WINdow©, where we've taken those best practices and created a tool that allows everyone to have that same level of success.

∘═╼═∘

GETTING THEM TO SIGN

When preparing to ask for signatures on a contract, be certain there are no unanswered questions or open issues. If you can think of any possible reason why the prospect would not sign, *then don't ask him or her to sign!* You risk losing valuable credibility when appearing too eager.

To prevent that situation from happening, be sure you check off most, if not all, of the items on what we call the "Ready to Sign Checklist" before asking the prospect to buy. Here are some examples of what belongs on it:

134

Ready to Sign Checklist

_____ I know all the decision makers and influencers in my prospect organization.

_____ I understand the issues and the financial impact for each one.

_____ I've met the buying criteria and proven my solutions' capabilities to each decision maker.

_____ I've woven a web of influence throughout my prospect's organization.

_____ I've connected the issues throughout the entire organization.

_____ I've talked to all the decision makers, and they have seen the final cost justification.

_____ The prospect has reviewed and approved the terms and conditions of my contract or proposal.

_____ All technical issues have been addressed and/or resolved.

_____ All legal issues have been addressed.

_____ Any vendor engagement and administrative issues have been addressed and resolved.

_____ I know who my competitors are, I know what they're offering, and I know what they're charging.

_____ I have differentiated my company from the competition and how they positioned me.

_____ I've cost justified our unique capabilities.

_____ I can't think of any reason not to ask for the signature.

Once you mentally go through that checklist and can confirm that all items are checked, then it's the right time to ask for the order.

Lastly, productive salespeople are fully prepared with a plan to stand firm so that they don't wing it. As a matter of fact, we've created a tool that enables salespeople to stand firm in final negotiations and win a majority of the time. We call that tool the "Stand FIRM© Action Plan." The acronym FIRM stands for:

Finance—Cost justification.

Impact—Consequences of delay/successes to be gained.

Request—What do you want the buyer to agree to?

Match—What will you offer in return?

SUMMARY OF KEY POINTS
(Chapter 15)

- Asking for the sale is an ongoing process from start to finish.

- Know the ten surefire ways to kill a sale.

- After you have established your credibility, using past successes to leverage for your future successes, you then get the prospect to start talking about his organization.

- Be sure to establish your personal credibility, as you want the prospect to want to buy from *you*.

- Think of yourself as a sales consultant or trusted advisor, not just a salesperson. You're helping prospects find solutions, not cramming your product or service down their throat.

- Create an entire library of customer success stories (in the Credibility WINdow© format) sharing some of the things you've helped other clients accomplish toward achieving their business goals.

- Be sure you can check off most if not all of the items on the "Ready to Sign Checklist" before asking the prospect to buy.

- Stand FIRM© in final negotiations.

16

Secrets of Successful Cross-Selling

Mark Ward, a veteran sales executive who weighed in earlier, also talks about how he has seen cross-selling work for him. In this case it was predicated on his being able to gain access to the right decision maker to make it work:

"This was when mobile telephone service was just becoming affordable. I was working for a major technology provider as the lead salesperson calling on a major wireless services provider. Our solution was for multiple millions of dollars over three years, and we were attempting to break into a market where switch-vendors such as Lucent, Nortel, and Ericcson dominated.

We had an ultimate goal of selling to this wireless services provider, selling solutions with this wireless services provider to joint clients, and selling through this wireless services provider.

Although the technical and functional teams preferred the other alternatives, the relationships we were able to establish with the president won the deal. This was one of the few times I have seen a senior-most executive work with their team to partner with a supplier and incorporate a business plan (including ROI) for the entire scope of the relationship."

Targeting and pursuing new prospects should always be a high priority for salespeople. But that is only part of the equation; another is tending to the existing client base and doing it with the intent of discovering new sales opportunities with these current customers.

Building new sales opportunities with existing customers, and thus new revenue streams, in this manner is what we call "cross-selling." An existing customer is already a "warm" prospect: You know the "key players" and the "key players" know you, so there are steps you can skip that are usually involved when first touching base with a new prospect. There's really no need for qualifying the prospect, introducing your services or products, or going on some hunting expedition to find who the decision makers are within the organization. There already is a mutual understanding and shared familiarity.

Establishing cross-selling sales relationships with a client is important because it allows you to gain a "bigger share of wallet" with that existing client without having to spend a ton of money on sales and marketing efforts.

Saying it another way, it costs a lot less in money and time to market to existing clients than it does to prospect to new clients. You always want to persist in doing the latter, but you don't want it to be your sole source of developing new business. For one thing, research shows that it's almost nine times more expensive to sell to somebody brand-new than it is to sell to an existing client.

Cross-selling to an existing client carries with it the luxury of being a simplified process. Fewer steps are involved. Among the steps or processes highlighted earlier in this book that probably can be skipped when cross-selling are the following:

- Getting the buyers through the Risk Stage of buying, which is the part where they start second-guessing themselves, wondering "What if it's not the right choice?" or "What if it doesn't work?" (See Chapter 1.) Now that they have a good history of doing business with you, they have confidence in you.

- Performing the due diligence via detailed research based on certain criteria so as to pare down a broad list of prospects into a shorter list of what are often called "selects." This process includes detailed scrutiny of information such as SICs (standard industry classifications) and vertical markets. (See Chapter 3.)

- Making the "dreaded" cold call over the telephone. (See Chapter 4.) Now you can just pick up the phone, using a warm-call approach to schedule an appointment.

- Navigating your way past gatekeepers and all that goes with it, such as having to send out those introductory direct-marketing letters, soliciting for follow-up contact, and then using your telephone script spoken in terms of trying to generate some interest as it relates to the letter. (See Chapter 5.)

141

Here's where salespeople can achieve their ROI on their sales efforts. By cross-selling, you can grow your territory and income. Here's why: It normally takes eighteen to twenty-four months before a customer becomes profitable. Most companies, perhaps even yours, load the entire cost of sales into the first year of a contract.

What that then means is that the more products and/or services that you can sell to that same company or organization, the bigger share of wallet you get. In addition, the more successful the relationship is, the less likely you are to lose that customer.

It's also important to document every successful cross-sell in your Credibility WINdow© library to win even more business!

○══◆══○

PUTTING CROSS-SELLING INTO MOTION

Refocus meetings are a good way to go back to existing clients and to work with them to uncover other needs that can be met by your products or services. The refocus meeting begins by thanking your customer for their business. Remind them again how much you appreciate them, and be sure to use your own words to best convey that to them.

Here's an example of what I say: "I'm not sure I've done as good a job as I should have understanding all the nuances of your business. I might not have shared all the capabilities that we have. During this refocus meeting, I'd like to make sure that I understand the mission-critical initiatives on your plate, introduce (or-reintroduce) you to our capabilities, and then spend the balance of our conversation where those points intersect."

If you say what I say, you'll be amazed how well you get engaged in business conversations that go well beyond whatever discussions you've had with them previously. If they've been a client for, say, five or more years, it's quite possible that those "mission-critical" initiatives (along with your capabilities) have changed. Refocus meetings allow you to go deeper and wider in the buyer's organization so you can weave an expanded web of impact.

Lastly, there likely are new personnel and decision makers in the mix. Refocus meetings are a good way to meet these new key people and press some flesh. By the time you leave, you should have some new answers to these same old questions, giving you the necessary information to uncover additional sales opportunities. They may introduce you to new departments, divisions, or subsidiaries that could buy from you.

Remember, use the Credibility WINdow© (Chapter 11) to improve your cross-selling success.

○══╪══○

CREATE A CROSS-SELL PIPELINE

This idea is a powerful one, as it causes you to create a whole new pipeline that runs parallel to your existing new-business or business-development pipeline.

To build a cross-sell pipeline, start by reviewing your existing client data base to find five to ten existing accounts that would be good targets. The goal here is to manage those five to ten accounts on a monthly basis. This also involves developing vertical markets, which is discussed in more detail in Chapter 20.

Of those ten accounts that you've identified, highlight five that could close in the next ninety days, and another five cross-sell opportunities that could close within the next twelve months.

The best way for you to be able to manage your cross-sell pipeline is to have some kind of automated reporting mechanism. Some examples would include ACT, Goldmine, Salesforce.com, Microsoft Outlook, etc. Whatever method you use, you must manage your cross-sell pipeline proactively.

SUMMARY OF KEY POINTS
(Chapter 16)

- Further scrutiny of your existing customer base will help you discover and then manage new sales opportunities with these current customers.

- Establishing cross-selling relationships with a customer allows you to gain "a bigger share of wallet" without having to spend a ton of money on marketing.

- It costs much less in money and time to market to existing clients than it does to prospect to new clients.

- Use the Credibility WINdow© to improve your cross-selling success.

- Use refocus meetings to identify additional opportunities.

- Cross-selling utilizes pipeline-development strategies discussed earlier. A good way to organize that is by going through your client data base and identifying five short-term prospects and five longer-term prospects.

17
Winning
RFP Strategies

For many salespeople, the road to new business starts with the receipt of an RFP (Request for Proposal), an RFQ (Request for Quote), or an RFI (Request for Information). At first glance, an RFP is proof positive that a company or organization is interested in your product or service. They just want to see what you can, or are willing to, do for them. In other words, they've chosen you to apply to be their vendor! It can become quite an ego booster! A willingness, even enthusiasm, to respond to an RFP is to be commended, but then comes the big question of whether or not it is worth the time, effort, and expense.

Not all RFPs are a harbinger of an impending sale, where a prospect is standing by at the other end with pen in hand, ready to sign the deal once you send a proposal. More often than not, a diabolical strategy is at work, especially if that RFP is coming at you from a (supposed) potential buyer you've never made contact with in the past.

We have found that there are four red flags that let you know that you are not the vendor of choice when you receive that RFP:

1. **When you get an unsolicited request to respond to a proposal.** When someone calls you out of the blue, sends you an e-mail, or happens to hit your Web site and is now saying, "We'd like you to respond to our proposal." Don't you see something fishy about that?

2. **The RFP has a list of requirements a mile long.** They say, "We need a product (or service) that does this, this, and this." The source of such an RFP didn't just dream up all those "requirements." Somebody else helped them create their requirements, and now you're working off their vision.

3. **You are given an artificially short timeframe to respond.** You get the call on Friday, they want a response on Monday, and they don't mean by 5 p.m. on Monday. The temptation is to work through the weekend because this huge opportunity dropped in your lap. In reality, the prospect is probably using you to negotiate with the vendor of choice. I suggest you think long and hard about responding to their request if you're not more than 50 percent sure you can win!

4. **Access to decision makers is limited, if there is any at all.** This is your clue from them, in this particular case, that they've already chosen somebody else with whom they want to do business but they are required by executive management to

solicit bids from two or three other companies in order to justify their decision. Whether they picked you to be column filler on their spreadsheet or picked your company randomly off the Web, they are just using you to justify who they have already selected as their vendor, or, worse yet, to "beat up" their existing vendor.

One of the basic tenets of making progress on a sale is gaining access to the decision makers. You must be able to speak to people who will influence the final outcome of the sale. If you end up getting passed around to lower-level members of the organization, or if your questions about the decision-making hierarchy are constantly rebuffed, the red flag is hitting you in the face.

Ask yourself: Are you "the vendor of choice" or just another supplier filling out a column on a spreadsheet? Even worse yet, what if you take the trouble to prepare an RFP response, laying out all your best stuff, and your prospect gives your proposal to the preferred vendor? Now the preferred vendor, your competitor, knows exactly what you're offering and what you're changing.

⚬══✦══⚬

DON'T VOLUNTEER TO BE COLUMN FILLER

Many organizations buy by sending out RFP's to multiple vendors. Put yourself in the shoes of the organization that has sent out RFPs and is now weighing vendors, using a spreadsheet to analyze potential vendors. The spreadsheet has columns highlighting each competing offering. This allows for the ease of comparison shopping. Here's how they might work their vendors in one sample scenario:

1. "Vendor 1 did a great job; turned our lights on; we really want to buy from him, but we have to get some other bids."

2. "So we go to Vendor 2, but they are missing a lot of the deliverables that Vendor 1 has, so we negotiate on terms and maybe they make a price concession."

3. "Then we go to Vendor 3, but they are missing even more of the deliverables that Vendor 1 has and, in fact, are not really competitive with Vendor 2, so if they want to win the business, they have to be the lowest price."

4. "We want to buy from Vendor 1, so we go back to them (the other two RFP responses in hand) and tell them, 'Vendor 2 gave us a small price concession and special terms, and Vendor 3 gave us a 20-percent price discount if we buy from them. We want to buy from you, but what can you do?' "

Always look for the red flags before this happens to you in your unwitting role as Vendor 2, 3, or 4, otherwise you'll end up as *Column Filler* on the spread sheet that awards the winning bid to your competitor.

<hr/>

QUALIFY THE RFP

We've heard it hundreds of times. Salespeople tell us the horrors of time, resources, and money wasted in responding to an RFP that, as it turned out, never had a chance in the first place. This was the result, after potentially spending tens of thousands of dollars or more to respond to just one RFP.

One of our clients a few years ago told us that it cost an average of $78,000 to respond to one RFP. In digging a little deeper with him to find out more about this experience, he said his company on average responded to two or three a month. When asked how many he had won, he said just two over the preceding twelve months. Obviously, he needed to tweak their strategy to somehow find a way to win more RFPs, or respond to fewer.

Another client went on to explain that his industry had changed over the previous twelve to eighteen months to where now RFPs had become a way of life, almost like a "damned if you do, damned if you don't" type of paradox. The problem was, he couldn't differentiate good opportunities from the bogus ones, leaving him no choice (he thought) but to respond to them all.

The most successful salespeople do two things to sort out the good RFPs from the bad before spending another dime or minute on any of them. First, they weigh each incoming RFP against the red-flag list referred to earlier. Second, they establish an RFP response strategy by asking themselves the following pointed questions:

- In terms of time, resources, and other materials, what does it cost my company to respond to an RFP?

- How many RFPs do we respond to a month?

- How many of those RFPs do we win?

151

- How many of those RFPs do we win at full contract value?

The information gained from these questions and the Red Flags (listed above) will allow you to establish your RFP Response Strategy so you can choose to respond only to those that you *know* you have a reasonable chance to win. A proper response to an RFP should be aggressive and intense, sometimes even costly, and no company can afford to waste all those resources on RFPs that are dead in the water even before you stick a toe in.

It is critical for you to determine as early as possible in the process if your prospects are going to take a serious look at your proposal, or are they going to use it only for the purpose of price-shopping their preferred supplier? Remember, if you end up in a situation in which you are only getting to deal on price without getting to establish your *value*, you face a losing proposition. Companies soliciting bids through multiple RFPs will routinely send *your* RFP to their supplier of choice simply to get that supplier to cave to terms more generous to the company. That means that your response is being used as a negotiating ploy that is of absolutely no benefit to you.

⸎

DON'T BE A PAWN

Make a commitment to set your organization apart from the competition to avoid being a pawn for another organization's advancement. You don't want your competition to make a profit at your expense! You can prevent this from happening by creating your RFP Response Strategy.

In today's business climate, purchasing agents and consultants are more and more prevalent at the end of "the buy cycle." Just as salespeople have traditionally been compensated for selling, these agents and consultants increasingly are being paid on the other end for how well they lower your price. With that trend still on the rise, here are some "best practices" you can employ when responding to an RFP to increase your chances of winning the business:

Winning RFP Strategies

- Get there first.
- Help create the requirements.
- Understand the decision-making process and the rules of engagement, and know who the account's key individuals are.
- Meet with the decision makers.

When you meet with the decision makers, you want to ask them:

- What are the company's strategic initiatives?
- What are the business goals they are hoping to achieve with this RFP?
- Who are the primary beneficiaries going to be?
- Know who you are competing against and what they are offering.
- Understand the "show stoppers" from your prospects' perspective. (They might have a lot of needs and wants, but find out beforehand the one or two show stoppers, meaning those things that, if you can't address them, will knock you out of the bidding.)

When executing winning RFP strategies, you need to identify and contact companies that use RFPs as a way of doing business (e.g. utility companies, government, etc.). By proactively contacting them, you might be able to help craft the RFP in such a way that increases your chance of winning.

SUMMARY OF KEY POINTS
(Chapter 17)

- Before you get too excited about an RFP, make sure you qualify the opportunity.

- One of the basic tenets of making a sale is gaining access to primary or secondary decision makers. You have to meet with the decision makers and discuss their strategic initiatives with them.

- Recognize the four red flags to watch for in an RFP, and never willingly give yourself up to be column filler.

- Establish an RFP response strategy so you can win more RFPs or respond to fewer.

- More and more companies are requiring their buyers to solicit at least three competitive bids from vendors to make sure they are seeing enough of what is out there to truly get the best deal.

- Make a commitment to differentiate your organization from the competition to avoid being a pawn for another organization's advancement.

18
Establishing Your Success Formula

There is a science to selling! Sales is a game; some might even call it a sport complete with rules and a scorecard. When all the numbers are added up, both the salesperson and the manager know the score immediately.

There are six quantifiable factors that a salesperson needs to identify and track on a monthly basis to ensure success and consistency:

1. What's your monthly quota in terms of sales dollars or gross revenue?

2. What's your average order size?

3. What's your close rate?

4. How long is your sales cycle?

5. How many qualified prospects must you have in your pipeline every month?

6. How many suspects do you need to talk to on a monthly basis to fill your qualified pipeline?

Let me give you an example. Let's say your sales quota is $5,000 per month, your average order size is $1,000, your close rate is 20% and your sales cycle is 60 days. If those numbers don't change, then you'd need 50 qualified prospects in your pipeline each month to achieve your quota. I came up with the number 50 because you need five sales of $1,000 to achieve your quota of $5,000 but you're only closing 20% of your sales (one in five) so you have to multiply five times five, which equals 25. Since your sales cycle is 60 days, you have to multiply the 25 times two to get to 50 prospects. To get 50 qualified prospects in your pipeline, you'll need to contact a lot of suspects. The number of suspects you need to talk to will vary by industry, but to play it safe you should contact three suspects for every qualified prospect you need to fill your pipeline.

Use this sample grid to establish your own Success Formula:

Sales Quota	$	/month
Average Order Size	$	
Close Rate		%
Sales Cycle		days
Qualified Prospects Needed		
Number of Suspects Needed		

By tracking your numbers and knowing how to interpret them, both a sales manager and a salesperson can see exactly what is working well, what isn't, and which areas offer the most potential for improvement. Used correctly and persistently, the salesperson's Success Formula can be used to establish guidelines on how to go about researching and finding new qualified prospects, how to better manage their time by identifying where efforts are being wasted, and how best to fine tune their scheduling of calls to either seek out more or do a more effective job of finding the right kind of prospects in the first place.

○══╋══○

CHANGING THE NUMBERS

It's one thing for a salesperson to know what his or her respective Success Formula is, but utilizing it is another matter. The good news is that salespeople can change those dynamics, those separate parts of the aforementioned Success Formula. For one thing, just as an example, they can sell bigger deals. That changes things dramatically. If nothing else changed except the order size, they would need fewer qualified prospects.

Taking it further, the salesperson can in fact not only increase the size of his or her average order, but also reduce the sales cycle by doing the following:

- Better profiling prospects upfront
- Selling additional products or services
- Selling multi-year deals

Again, it's all a numbers game. Once you can track

159

and interpret the numbers, improving your sales performance becomes a quantifiable activity, as in, "If I just do *this*, then *that* will happen." It's like the old Willie Sutton line, referring to the notorious bank robber of years ago. When the authorities finally captured Willie and sat him down to interrogate him, they asked him, "Gee, Willie, why do you rob banks?" He responded, "Because that's where the money is."

For salespeople, the money is in selling bigger deals to bigger companies, more quickly!

POST-CALL DEBRIEFING

To improve your Success Formula by getting more and bigger sales out of it, be prepared to answer the following Post-Call Debriefing questions:

1. Who are the key decision makers?
2. What are their needs or critical business issues?
3. What are the reasons for their needs?
4. What is the organizational impact?
5. What is the financial impact?
6. What is their vision of a solution?
7. What is the decision-making process at the company?
8. What is the next step, and by whom, and when?

The answers to these eight questions will help you leverage your chances of winning the business. It's vital that salespeople document and recap their activities, both internally and externally. This goes along with the idea of taking notes as discussed in Chapter 14.

Keeping track of this information is necessary so you will be able to send an e-mail or regular letter—which we call a "VALU Letter" or "Recap Letter"—to the prospect to help move the sale along. Again, documenting what is discussed is very effective when it comes to improving your Success Formula, plus it keeps you in alignment with the buyer.

○━━◆━━○

MAKING IT WORK

Your Success Formula will work as long as you execute and internalize it. It begins with qualifying enough prospects, and qualifying them according to the right criteria you have established when it comes to developing your pipeline.

That's why the measurement is so important. Salespeople are better off making fewer cold calls and fewer telemarketing calls, and they have better success with them than just that whole dialing-for-dollars concept. That churn-and-burn mentality is for telemarketers who deal in a numbers game and aren't as skilled as salespeople, even though the latter—and that includes you—sometimes get tarred with that same brush wielded by prospects. That's why it's so important that we behave differently.

○━━◆━━○

161

SUMMARY OF KEY POINTS
(Chapter 18)

- Sales are always measurable, and they can be quantified in a number of different ways that include average order size, a salesperson's success rate in closing sales, and how many contacts with prospects it takes to produce a sale.

- The salesperson's Success Formula gives him a measurable base from which he can shoot for improvement, knowing almost exactly what he needs to do to accomplish his goals.

- The salesperson can increase the size of the average order and reduce the sales cycle by better profiling prospects upfront, selling products or services for a bigger share of wallet, and improving the close rate.

- To sell bigger deals, always answer the post-call debriefing questions after every call.

19

Outsmarting
the Competition

Have you ever lost a sale that you were sure you were going to win? If so, then you were probably outsmarted by your competition. The reason I say that is that you thought you were going to win, and the prospect never indicated that you were going to lose!

Characteristics of
"Strategic" Competitors

- They offer similar products or services to yours.
- You compete with them all the time.
- You've lost business to them in the past.
- They have a similar infrastructure and financial strength.
- They are already in all or most of your markets.
- Your market views them as your competitor.
- They have a similar strategy or vision.

Pay heed: Even if you don't know who your competitors are, more than likely they know *you*. Knowing that should keep you on your toes. You need to make sure you stay at least one step ahead of your competition.

THE GOLDEN RULE

The golden rule for outsmarting the competition is to have a wealth of prospect knowledge. Such knowledge includes knowing the names and titles of key players in your prospect's organization, the industry and market that your prospect serves, and the competition that you are likely to encounter.

Here are the Eight Keys to Outsmarting Your Competition:

1. Create a competitive advantage in your marketplace.

2. Establish and implement a consistent proactive account-planning process.

3. Develop product capability and product application knowledge.

4. Effectively target your prospects.

5. Know the secrets of how organizations buy.

6. Know how to sell to different buyer personalities.

7. Sell value, not price.

8. Stand FIRM© during the final negotiations.

Today's top salespeople spend ample time being introspective about their selling successes and their selling challenges. They look at how their industry has

164

changed over the previous eighteen to twenty-four months from both a positive and negative perspective. A positive perspective could include creation of unique products, more "need" for your kind of products or services, or weakening competition. A negative perspective could include increased competition, a poor economy, or budget cuts.

> *The golden rule for outsmarting the competition is to have a wealth of prospect knowledge.*

They also look at how their marketplace has changed over that same period of time—which stores or businesses have opened or closed, whether there has been an increase in hiring or an increasing number of layoffs, or if decisions are being made quickly or if there have been delays in decision making.

They also identify the selling challenges they have faced over the past eighteen to twenty-four months. Those could include the inability to connect with senior-level decision makers or a failure to get decision makers to take action.

One way to address these changes and challenges is to understand how your prospects view your company as it relates to your competition. We know for a fact that all companies have specific needs in order to be successful in their own marketplace.

We also know that these companies have a perception—right or wrong—about your ability to address their specific needs versus your competition. In some cases, they believe that your capabilities are stronger than your competitor's capabilities in addressing their needs. These are the contracts you should win. In other cases, the company perceives that you don't match up.

Either way, your job is to maximize your strengths and minimize your weaknesses to increase the chances of your success.

To "win," you will have to change their perception of you, your product offering, and/or your company. It's getting tougher all the time to do this, though, as more often salespeople are getting less face time in front of their prospects. You need to be nimble and able to move quickly and persuasively at the same time.

S.W.O.T. ANALYSIS

You've heard of SWAT teams, the special police units that get called in to handle the critical threats on the street faced by our men and women in blue. Well, our SWOT Analysis does not involve wearing body armor or carrying advanced weaponry, but it does help our own force, the sales force, better understand who's lurking in the marketplace and, as importantly, how the market perceives your company versus your competition.

Most people are familiar with the term SWOT Analysis. In many companies, their marketing departments perform a SWOT Analysis on a regular basis. The acronym SWOT stands for:

> Strengths
> Weaknesses
> Opportunities
> Threats

THE TRUTH HURTS (AND IT HELPS)

The SWOT Analysis is usually performed by the marketing department, giving an internal look at the marketplace. What does your own organization do well and what do you not do so well? The answers comprise a list of your strengths and weaknesses as well as what opportunities and threats are out there.

I'm suggesting that the sales force and management team need to work together to discover how the market perceives you. Do they see you as stronger than the competition or weaker than the competition as it relates to satisfying their needs? This entails "stepping outside" yourselves, observing with a detached point of view that allows you to see yourselves as others see you.

This is not the time to be defensive or apologetic; all you are trying to do is gather the kind of intelligence on your company that will make you stronger. The more objectively that you can point the viewfinder at yourself, the better the analysis of your own organization will be.

By looking at the "S" and the "W" from the prospects' perspective, you'll get a truer picture of market perception. While it might not be true, *the fact is that their perception is your reality*. On the other hand, the "O" and "T" lists should come from your own perspective: Ask yourself, "What could we do that would hurt the competition in the marketplace?" And, "What might they do that would hurt us?"

One point that I'd like to caution you about is the following: *Perceptions change only when new experiences or new information is received over an extended period of time.* You can tell your prospects that your customer service function has improved, but until they experience that improvement for themselves and then actually believe that it is sustainable, their perception will not change.

> *One of my clients, Hunter McCarty of Tennessee-based R. J. Young (which sells large office equipment such as copiers and printers), said he had just been through a stretch of about forty-five days in which he had encountered several instances of having to forgo the familiar relationship-oriented sale in favor of a barebones commodity-like sale.*
>
> *"Buyers are becoming more savvy as they have more opportunity to gather information on their own, such as going to the Internet to get all the specs for the different models of a piece of equipment they are looking to buy," McCarty says. "Even the smaller companies buying fewer units are doing this. Those vendors who are the best at answering questions about value and service are the only ones getting face time."*

THE FIVE-P STRATEGY

The best salespeople have an Account Strategy that we call the Five-P Strategy to target a specific prospect. It involves the following:

The Five-P Strategy

1. Position

   a. How do you want this account to know you?

   b. How will you enhance or change their perception of you?

   c. What is the timeline for changing their perception?

   d. What is your unique value proposition? Which is to say, what is it that you do that your competition can't do, doesn't do, or won't do in the marketplace?

2. Placement

   a. You need to know the job titles and functional areas you want to penetrate at this particular account.

   b. You also need to target the markets, segments, or divisions within the company you want to sell to.

3. Products

   a. Identify the products or services you want to sell to this account.

4. Price

   a. Identify your pricing philosophy for this account.

   b. Do you want to be the low-cost leader? The high-price player? The value-added seller? Can you offer market-building pricing? Can you give special pricing to vertical markets?

   c. Identify your gross-margin requirements.

5. Promotion

   a. Identify how you will promote your product or service. Options include direct sales, indirect sales, providing subject-matter experts, PowerPoint presentations or demonstrations, pilot programs, etc.

〜✦〜

GETTING PROSPECTS TO SWITCH

Many of your prospects are already buying from a competitor a product or service that matches yours or is at least quite similar. Take that to the bank as a positive for you. It means they are already fully qualified—there's no guesswork involved as to determining whether or not they are interested in your products. They are, even if they don't know it yet. The important thing is that you *do* know this, and it's time for you to go after them.

> *What is it that you do that your competition can't do, doesn't do, or won't do in the marketplace?*

All you have to do is prove that the benefits they will receive from you and your product or service are greater than what they are getting now from their current vendor. Here are five suggestions on how to make such a prospect work with you:

1. Query the prospect regarding satisfaction with the competitor's product and service. You have to know all that you can about your competitor before you can win business from them. What does the prospect like about the present supplier? Are there any areas that could be improved? Once you start uncovering advantages for you, start bringing these into the discussion.

2. Sell the favorable difference(s) *you can offer*. Even if you can't beat the competitor's price, you have plenty of other possible advantages, such as financing, delivery, service, quality, assistance with set-up, etc.

170

3. Use the Credibility WINdow©. Bring out the endorsements and testimonials from your satisfied clients or customers.

4. Let them try your product or service. This is a compromise many prospects will jump at, even if it is a last resort for you. So what? Once you have proven yourself, then you can ask for their business.

5. Always assume a smart competitor is chasing after your own customers. It works both ways. Stay alert to customer needs, and make every effort to continue to satisfy them, even surprise or delight them. *Remember, you don't have to satisfy all of your customers … just the ones you want to keep!*

COMPETITIVE STRATEGIES

While there are many types of competitive strategies, I'd like to focus in on three. They are the Reactive Strategy, the Proactive Strategy, and the Preemptive Strategy. Let's take a look at them:

1. Reactive Strategy: Unfortunately, many companies and many salespeople use or employ a reactive strategy. The competition does "this," so they do "that." The market does "this," so they do "that." Their client does "this," so they do "that." They "react " only when they are forced to. It's very tactical, which is not a good way to establish long-term value or long-term relationships.

2. Proactive Strategy: A proactive strategy means that we take action and get there before the competition

> *Sell the favorable difference(s) you can offer. Even if you can't beat the competitor's price, you have plenty of other possible advantages, such as financing, delivery, service, quality, assistance with set-up, etc.*

or other factors force us to act. We start taking people into new markets, developing new products, and creating new capabilities in advance of the competition.

3. Preemptive Strategy: A preemptive strategy means that we take action to be on the cutting edge. We are the pacesetters. Not only do we get there first, but no matter who enters our space afterward, they're going to have a hard time competing. The best example I can give you is Southwest Airlines, which has now been in business about thirty-five years. When they first came along with their short-hop, no-frills service, the big airlines just kind of laughed at them. Business/Market experts said that Southwest would never make it.

Well, here it is all these years later, and Southwest is the only airline that has maintained profitability, even through 9/11 and other difficult economic times.

Southwest Airlines is a perfect example of creating a preemptive strategy. Here are some selected decisions that they made to establish a competitive advantage:

- They went to secondary and tertiary markets so they wouldn't have to pay the exorbitant gate fees. That meant they were able to go to places that people wanted to visit, and they were less congested.

- They bought only one type of aircraft, so they didn't have parts or training issues. A pilot would fly the same kind of aircraft regardless of the

172

route he or she flew. By buying the same type of aircraft, they didn't have maintenance or parts issues either.

- They created employee ownership. All of the employees actually are owners of the airline, so they have a vested interest.

- They did fuel hedging, buying fuel at a lower rate by committing to certain volumes for long periods of time.

- They became experts in twenty-minute turns. That means they were able to get a plane turned and back up in the air in twenty minutes. None of the bigger carriers could do that.

> *Remember, you don't have to satisfy all of your customers ... just the ones you want to keep!*

- They did not assign seating. That makes it quicker for them to load the airplane.

- They carried cargo in the belly of the plane to share the operational costs with the passengers.

In looking at air travel today, we can see that many other discount airlines have come and gone, but no one has been able to compete with Southwest Airlines because of their preemptive strategy.

SUMMARY OF KEY POINTS
(Chapter 19)

- Losing a sale at the last minute is a sign that you have been outsmarted by a competitor.

- The golden rule for outsmarting the competition is to have a wealth of *prospect knowledge*.

- A SWOT analysis identifies the market-place perception of your company and assesses four areas: Strengths, Weaknesses, Opportunities, and Threats.

- Successful salespeople utilize a Five-P account strategy that involves position, placement, products, price, and promotion.

- To get prospects to switch from using competitors as vendor, you must prove that the benefits they will receive from you and your product or service are greater than what they are getting currently from their current vendors.

- Focus on the Reactive Strategy, the Proactive Strategy, and the Preemptive Strategy to further your competitive strategy.

- *Remember, you don't have to satisfy all of your customers ... just the ones you want to keep!*

20

Creating
Target Opportunity
"Hit Lists"

The most successful salespeople create Target Opportunity "Hit Lists" including competitive take-away accounts, large opportunities in geographic markets, and selected vertical-market prospects. The fact is that you don't have to sell too many of these accounts to make your year!

One of the most common problems new and ambitious salespeople create for themselves comes from trying to be all things to all markets. They know what it means to target prospects, but their field of fire goes far and wide. They take aim at anyone and anything that has a pulse and a mailing address and/or telephone number. They do so without distinguishing a viable prospect from one that is a poor suspect at best.

Successful salespeople, in targeting prospects and developing their pipelines, constantly perform careful research and analysis upfront to eliminate suspects. They do this so that they can uncover the best prospects before they start sending out letters and trying to make appointments.

The segments you market to should be those that most closely resemble your best customers today. In effect, you want to penetrate specific vertical markets, which are the same, or similar, markets of your best existing customers.

One way to segment your market is to use either Standard Industrial Classification (SIC) codes or North American Industry Classification System (NAICS) codes. These codes allow you to sort through names of companies that fit your marketing profile. Make sure you aim your prospecting laser in the right direction.

There are many Websites (e.g. Dun and Bradstreet, Experian, InfoUSA, etc.) in addition to various reference books you can refer to for these codes, but keep in mind that most Websites with truly comprehensive databases are going to charge you a fee to access those databases. It's well worth the price to get reliable prospecting information.

There's another approach to determining which organizations fit your profile. Take a hard look at your competitors and see what kinds of companies and organizations they have listed as references on their Web sites. A good hour or so studying their Websites will unveil a surprising amount of prospecting information. At the same time, assume your competitors are doing the very same thing, eyeballing your Website to see what kind of paths you are beating down. Remember, two can play that game, so work it to your advantage.

Successful salespeople, in targeting prospects and developing their pipelines, constantly perform careful research and analysis upfront to eliminate suspects. They do this so that they can uncover the best prospects before they start sending out letters and trying to make appointments.

As illustrated earlier in the book (Chapter 3), it is advised

176

that you target your prospects by determining what your best prospects look like. Know the answers to the following questions to help you profile your prospects:

1. What industries are they in?
2. What kind of products or services do they buy from me?
3. What kind of revenue streams do they have?
4. How many employees do they have?
5. How many locations do they have?

IDENTIFYING VERTICAL MARKETS

You must be able to identify prospects in specific vertical markets that you can sell to in the near term. Think how much easier your selling life would be if your company were *the supplier* for the financial services industry or the pharmaceutical industry.

ACCOUNT PLANNER

To create Target Opportunity "Hit Lists," you need to be an ace at your own administrative work, keeping track of all this accumulated profile information and your various methods of prospecting. Most sales professionals are not really good at the administrative part of the job. If you are one of those, you need to use technology to your advantage. Look into contact-management software such as Outlook, ACT, Goldmine, or even Web-based products such as salesforce.com.

One tool that we have devised and that is particularly useful is what we call the Account Planner. It is used to compile the precise kind of information you need to track in order to properly identify potential vertical markets. An example of the Account Planner is on the following page. The major subject areas to be filled out for each prospect include:

- Account Background (to include industry, products, and competitors)

- Account Profile (annual sales, percentage of market share, current annual revenue with this account, potential annual revenue with this account)

- Key Contacts—identifies Influencer, Decision Maker, End User, and Approver

- Relationships with Competitors

- My Sales Objectives

Too often, when turnover occurs in a sales organization, the new salesperson is put at a disadvantage because the former salesperson didn't document important account information in writing and, consequently, all the account information left when he or she left! The purpose of the Account Planner form is to keep the most important information in an organized, electronic format. When done correctly, new salespeople are able to hit the ground running. In addition, internal partners such as customer service, IT, marketing, etc. can have access to key information about a specific prospect or client.

Account Planner

Sales Person:	Date:	Prospect:
Account Name:	% to Close:	Existing Customer:
Address:		

Account Background	Industry: Products: Competitors:		
Account Profile	Annual Sales: % of Market Share: Current Annual Revenue with this account: Potential Annual Revenue with this account: Other:		
Key Contacts	Influencer (I) Decision Maker (D) End User (E) Approver (A)		
	Name/Job Title	Telephone/E-mail	Issues/Needs/Notes
IDEA			
IDEA			
IDEA			
IDEA			
IDEA			
IDEA			
IDEA			
Relationships with Competitors			
My Sales Objectives			

SUMMARY OF KEY POINTS
(Chapter 20)

- The successful salesperson targets prospects in small, well-qualified numbers instead of trying to be all things to all markets.

- A good way to target your prospects is by finding those who closely resemble your current customers. Another good way is by looking at those accounts your competitors are targeting.

- A good salesperson is a master at his own administrative work, keeping track of accumulated profile information to track his customers, prospects and his own various methods of prospecting.

- Productive selling organizations establish a vertical market program, targeted account "hit lists," and other segmentation efforts so they can measure their progress on a regular basis.

- The account planner is used to compile the precise kind of information you need to track in order to properly identify potential vertical markets.

- SIC and NAICS codes are indispensable sources of market-segment information.

21
Creating a Productive Selling Zone® in Review

Salespeople who create their own Productive Selling Zone® are able to:

- Identify decision makers early in the sales process (versus selling to someone who can't buy)

- Engage those decision makers in strategic, proactive conversations (versus reactive, tactical conversations)

- Differentiate themselves and their company from their competition (versus being viewed as a commodity)

- Sell value, not price

- Deliver consistent results on a monthly basis

- Shorten their sales cycles

- Increase their average order size

- Maintain the integrity of their pricing

- Stand FIRM© in negotiations

Organizations that create a Productive Selling Zone® for their sales teams are able to:

- Create a customer-focused strategy that permeates the entire sales organization

- Establish standardized processes to proactively engage decision makers on a consistent basis

- Outsmart their competition by positioning proposals and RFPs to their advantage

- Sell products/services at full market value, without having to discount

- Establish a standardized process to *accurately* forecast new business and revenue performance

- Improve the size and the quality of their new business and cross-sell pipelines

- Increase the number of salespeople *at* or *above* plan

- Reduce turnover in their sales force

It all comes down to execution! To create your own Productive Selling Zone®, make sure that you internalize the tools, processes, and concepts from this book, and start using them right away. May this year become your most productive selling year ever!

— John Boyens

Boyens Group®
Core Competencies

- Assessments of people, processes, and programs
- Custom design and facilitation of Sales Productivity programs
- Custom design and facilitation of Management Effectiveness programs
- Leadership Development
- Executive Coaching
- Coaching at the salesperson level
- Certification programs
- Keynote addresses and guest speaking engagements
- Facilitation of customer feedback sessions ("online" and "in person")
- Sales compensation consulting
- Facilitation of competitive market strategy sessions (at both the account and the market level)
- Business consulting
- Multimedia Continuing Education Programs

- Accelerated Sales Audio Program ... CD's include the following:
  * "Making Money — How to Create a Successful Business Plan"
  * "Coaching for Optimal Performance"
  * "The Roadmap to Goal Setting"
  * "Making Time Work for You"
  * "Focusing on Customer Retention"
  * "Acquiring New Customers"
  * "Minimizing Turnover"
  * "Outsmarting the Competition"
  * "Selling Over the Phone"
  * "The Secrets of Building Rapport"
  * "Referrals = Success"
  * "Maximizing Your Tradeshow Budget"

Selected Boyens Group® programs include:

SALES PRODUCTIVITY

- Creating a Productive Selling Zone®
- Techniques of World Class Sellers
- Igniting Performance
- Practical Application Lab

MANAGEMENT EFFECTIVENESS

- The Five Fatal Flaws of Management
- Executive Sales Leadership
- Techniques of World Class Managers
- Coaching for Optimal Performance
- Managing for Results

BUSINESS STRATEGY

- Market Action Plan
- Account Strategy Action Plan

Selected speaking engagement topics include:

- *Creating a Productive Selling Zone®*
- *Coaching for Optimal Performance*
- *The Art of Leadership*
- *Ten Ways to Screw Up a Sale*
- *Five Fatal Flaws of Management*
- *The Three R's of Turnover*
- *Managing Change with Minimal Disruption*
- *Outsmarting the Competition*
- *Igniting Performance*
- *Everything is in a State of Flux, including Status Quo*
- *Top Ten Ways to Guarantee High Turnover*
- *Exceeding Customer Expectations*
- *Seven Characteristics of the Right Customer Service Attitude*

We also offer an electronic newsletter that is delivered the first month of every quarter. It includes a sales productivity tip of the quarter, a sales management tip of the quarter, and a spotlight on a Top Performer along with other valuable reinforcement tools. The newsletter is free, so please call (615) 776-1257 or visit us on the Web at www.boyens.com to sign up.

The Author

John Boyens has dedicated his business life to maximizing the productivity of sales processes for over 30 years. During his career in corporate America, John led national sales, service, and marketing organizations to consistently increase sales productivity, improve market share, accelerate revenue performance, and deliver bottom-line profit results.

His proven track record as an executive sales leader with several *Fortune* 1000 companies as well as his research on over 15,000 salespeople and sales managers across the globe uniquely qualified him to form the Boyens Group® in 1998.

John's expertise in sales, sales management, and business strategy keeps him in demand as a guest speaker, facilitator, workshop leader, and business consultant. He has addressed thousands of business executives and salespeople in a variety of formats, delivering customized programs on such topics as: *"Outsmarting the Competition," "Igniting Performance," "Sharpening the Axe," "Techniques of World Class Sellers," "Creating a Productive Selling Zone®," "Coaching for Optimal Performance," "Techniques of*

World Class Managers," "*Managing for Results,*" and "*Executive Sales Leadership.*"

John is the author of several audio CD series, including *Techniques of World Class Sellers, Accelerated Sales Audio Program,* and *Creating a Productive Selling Zone®.* In addition John is the co-author of *Real World Sales Strategies that Work.*

John is a graduate of North Central College and is an active member of the National Speakers Association, Professional Speakers Bureau International, the International Speakers Network and Sales, Marketing Executives International, and the International Franchise Association.

The Boyens Group® has a network of Associates throughout the U.S. who have earned their living as salespeople, managing sales organizations and implementing sales processes.

In addition, the Boyens Group® leverages its relationships with a select group of presidents, CEOs, vice presidents of sales, and vice presidents of marketing, who act as advisors on such topics as market conditions, industry trends, and predictions for the future.